BROKEN VOICES

'Untouchable' Women Speak Out

Valerie Mason-John

With much
Kindness
Valerie
x ♡ 4

Karunadeepa

India Research Press

BROKEN VOICES
'Untouchable' Women Speak Out
Valerie Mason-John

2008

India Research Press
Flat No. 6, Khan Market, New Delhi - 110 003
Ph.: 24694610; Fax : 24618637
www.indiaresearchpress.com
contact@indiaresearchpress.com; bahrisons@vsnl.com

The author's research was funded by
Arya Tara Mahila Trust, Pune, India and Arts Council, England

ISBN-13 digit : 81-8386-07-37
ISBN-10 digit : 978-81-8386-07-34

Printed for India Research Press at Focus Impressions, New Delhi.

For my Indian sisters from the lowest castes of India.
You are my heroines, my teachers.
Thank you for your courage and inspiration.

About the Author

Valerie Mason-John is second generation Black British. She was born in Cambridge and grew up in orphanages. She began her career as a journalist and covered a range of stories from Australian Aboriginal Land Rights, Black deaths in custody, to prisoners in Maghaberry Prison, Northern Ireland. Her work has been published in the *Guardian*, *The Voice* and *The Morning Star*. She has written and produced several plays, and is the author of five books. The first two document the lives of African and Asian women in Britain, her third is a collection of poetry, prose and plays, the fifth a self-awareness manual *Detox Your Heart,* on working with anger, fear and hatred. Her debut novel, *Borrowed Body* won the MIND book of the year award 2006. In 2007 she was awarded an honorary doctorate from the University of East London for her lifetime achievements and contribution to the African Diaspora through literature and the arts. She also won the Windrush Achievement Awards – Arts and Community Pioneer 2000, and the inaugural Shorelines/ Cutlureword first chapter competition. She continues to write both non-fiction and fiction and works as a trainer in anger management and conflict resolution. She divides her time between England and North America.

Contents

Acknowledgements

This book was inspired by Kurunamaya who has dedicated the last ten years of her life helping to empower women from the 'ex untouchable' castes of India. I have tremendous gratitude and admiration for her relationships with these women and felt inspired to help with her vision, of documenting the lives of some of the lowest caste women living in India.

I am indebted to the women who opened up their hearts, and homes to me, who cooked for me, who welcomed me into their families and told their stories. To the village women who let me work side by side in the rice fields and taught me traditional Indian dances, inviting me back home as their guest of honour. Thank you to the president of the Buddhist Society of India, Meera Ambedkar, the Mayor of Pune Rajani Ravindra Tribhuvan, the political leader Sulekha Kumbhare, the renowned writer Urmila Pawar, union activist Kusum Gangurde, Professor Nisha Shende and artist Jidnysa Anil Kedari for agreeing to be included in this important book.

This book would not have been possible if women had not taken time off from work and volunteered to translate for me. I am in awe of all of you who speak such good English and have never stepped outside India. Thank you Dr. Swati Barathe, Malati Wankhede, Dr. Manda Mune, Madhavi Maitreya, Dr. Sujata Gaikwad. Mrs. Indu Vinod Tembhurne. Mrs. Rekha Manoj Tambe, Vaishali Vasnik, Yogini Shende and to the men who helped translate too—Manidhamma, Vivekamitra, Mr. Kuringivalavan, Mr. Sakthivel. Thank you so much to

Saibrau the rickshaw driver from Nagpur with all your many contacts. And to all the staff at Pune hostel, to Sujata Waghmare, Karunaprabha and Karunadipa.

Thank you to Sangharakshita, Shraddhajoyti, Maitir-pushpa, Mangesh Dahiwale, Sudarshan, Subhuti, Kumarjeev and many others for their critical feedback. Thank you to the team at the Arya Tara Mahila Trust, especially Vasundhara Shende who accommodated me with all my needs and requests. And to the male community living at the Bhaja Retreat Centre who looked after me so well while writing the book, especially Arunavajra, Ratnasambhava and Suchandara

Thank you to Val Witonska for proof reading my early drafts and to Vidayadevi for editing it into a presentable manuscript that I could approach publishers with. Thank you to Vanadanjoyti for compiling a glossary. Thank you to Satyadarshin for donating his time and creativity for the cover design and to Dhammarati for gifting me with one of his images. Also a big thank you to Jnanasiddhi for introducing me to Tara Press, and supporting the book.

Thank you to Dada Mandreka, Dillip and Raja Sekhar Vundra, Vijay Mankar, for your overwhelming support and help. Thank you to Cheryl Kehoe for keeping me sane while I was living, breathing and eating some of these moving stories. To Nina Rapi, Georgina Edema and Jacky Mollinson for your phone calls that kept me in touch with my life back in England. Thank you to Tara Press and India Research for believing in this book, especially Deborah Smith and Anuj Bahri. Finally thank you to all the people I haven't named. I have much gratitude for the support, and belief that you have in this book.

Glossary

Ambedkar	–	Dr. Bhimrao Ramji
Ambidave	–	also spelt Ambivade, Ambedkar's home village, another form of the God Shankar.
Arunthathiyar	–	Tamil Nadu Dalit group
Avdhadut	–	a living deva
Baba	–	Hindu saint
Babasaheb	–	Honorific term for Ambedkar-Dr. Bhimrao Ramji
Bahujan Samaj Party	–	political party formed by Kamshi Ram in 1984
Balwadi	–	Kindergarten
Bhagavad-Gita	–	Hindu scripture
Bhakari	–	flat corn bread made by village people
Bhante	–	Urgyen Sangaharakshita
Bidi	–	traditional Indian leaf cigarette
Bhikku	–	Buddhist monks
Bindi	–	coloured spot worn in centre of women's foreheads
Bolai	–	tribe from Corku
Brahma	–	Hindu god
Brahmins	–	born from the mouth of God
Caste certificate	–	entitling SC people to reservation posts
Casteism	–	caste prejudice
Chai	–	spicy tea
Chamar	–	cobbler caste from the Uttar Pradesh region
Chappals	–	sandals
Chaturvarnya,		
Corku	–	tribal area

Dana	–	charity
Dalit	–	political title originally used by the followers of Ambedkar, but has now become one of the contemporary terms of identifying the ex 'Untouchable' population as a whole
Dalit Panthers	–	derived from Black Panthers in America
Deeksha (diksha)	–	ordinations
Deeksha bhumi	–	place of Ambedkar's conversion
Depressed classes	–	British name for Dalit under British rule
Deshmukh, Dr. Panjabrao	–	colleague of Ambedkar
Deva	–	goddess
Devadasi	–	women working in Hindu temple
Dhamma	–	the teachings of the Buddha
Dhammacarini	–	woman ordained in TBMSG
Dhammamitra	–	committed friend of TBMSG
Dharavi	–	the largest slum in Asia
Dimadi and tunatuna	–	traditional musical instruments
Diwali	–	Hindu New Year Festival
Dowry	–	given by woman's family to husband's family at marriage
Endogamy	–	caste rules for marriage
Ganesh	–	Ganpati
Ganpati	–	Hindu elephant god
Ghee	–	clarified butter
Ghutka	–	an addictive tobacco
Harijans	–	Mahatma Gandhi's name for untouchables
Hindustan	–	term used to describe Indian national identity (1917)
Independent Labour Party ILP	–	Ambedkar's first political party
Intercaste marriage	–	marriage outside one's own caste or *jati*
Jagran	–	wedding programme of dance and music

Jagari	–	traditional dance of the gods
Jai Bhim	–	Ambedkarite greeting composed from his name Ramji Bhimrao
Jati	–	subcaste
Kabir	–	poet
Karma	–	in mainstream Hindu philosophy has been interpreted as one's deeds, condition and caste will determine lives yet to be lived. This belief has discriminated against the ex Untouchables and Sudras. However, Karma literally meaning action. The Buddha taught that all things are dependent on conditions and that actions which arise from conditions have consequences. These consequences may mature now or many Buddhists believe in a future life. Unskilful actions of body, speech and mind based on conditioning factors of greed, hatred and delusion are said to lead to suffering. While skilful actions based on kindness, generosity and wisdom help one to be more in alignment with how things really are and lead to greater contentment. Karma is misunderstood to mean not only the action but also the results. It is also frequently misunderstood to be a form of fatalism.
Khandaba	–	Hindu god normally associated with the Scheduled Castes
Kshatriyas	–	second varna - born from the arms and hands of Brahma
Lakh	–	100,000
Lakshami (Lakshmi)	–	Hindu goddess of money
Mahar	–	Untouchable subcaste in Maharashtra, village servants. Ambedkar's subcaste
Mahatma Jatirao Phule	–	the father of the social revolution in India
Maitri Bhavana	–	the meditation of loving kindness

Mangalasutra	–	necklace of gold/black beads for married women
Mangs	–	subcaste
Manu	–	author of Manusmriti
Manusmriti	–	Manu, the law giver, wrote a treatise based on the verses in the Chaturvarnya
Maratha	–	upper caste subcaste of Maharashtra
Marathi	–	language spoken in Maharashtra
Matangs	–	Dalit subcaste
Metta	–	friendship
Murli		
Nomadic tribes	–	
Other Backward Castes	–	OBC
Pali Canon		
Pallass	–	Tamil Nadu Dalit group
Panchama	–	fifth varna for Harijans
Panchayat	–	village council
Paraya	–	Tamil Nadu Dalit group
Parvati	–	wife of Shankar (Hindu god)
Patwari	–	a government representative
People's Education Society	–	started colleges for Dalits
Puja	–	devotional practice
Purusha Sukta	–	the 19th hymn
Ramayan	–	Hindu scripture
Rangoli	–	pattern made outside the front door on the ground
Reservations		positive discrimination in schools and workplaces for low caste groups
Rukhmai	–	Hindu goddess
Rupee / paisa	–	Indian currency
Sadhus	–	Hindu wandering priests
Saint Gadge Maharaj Mission	–	Hostel charity for girls
Sangha	–	the community of practising Buddhists
Sangharakshita	–	venerable Urgyen – founder of the TBMSG

Sarapanch	–	the leader of the village political body (head of panchayat)
Sati	–	burning of a widow on her husband's funeral pyre
Scheduled Caste	–	ex 'Untouchable'
Scheduled Caste Federation	–	Ambedkar's first political party
Scheduled Tribes	–	
Shiv Sena	–	Hindu political party
Smriti (Manusmriti)	–	Hindu scripture written by Manu
S. N. Goenka	–	Vipassana teacher
Stupas	–	A spiritual monument – when a great teacher dies in India, a stupa is erected to symbolise the enlightened mind

Introduction

I first went to India in 1987, as an international correspondent covering the situation of bonded labourers, those who were indebted to high caste farmers and working as slaves. The majority of these people were from the ex 'Untouchable' castes. As a tourist I visited the extremes of India. One moment I was in one of the top hotels in Mumbai at a Bollywood party, and the next I walked several floors down back into poverty on the streets that I could hardly describe. I found myself loving India and hating it too, with all its contradictions. I loved India because it was the first country I had ever been to where my skin colour made me part of the majority, and I hated it because the shade of my skin and my gender were the two things that would have made my life very different if I had been born there. For Indian people, to see a dark-skinned female in Western clothing was an anomaly then. No doubt they thought I should have been covered from head to toe, at home attending to my domestic duties.

There are fair, brown and black Indians, and the majority of those who are brown or black belong to the Dalit (ex 'Untouchable' caste) community, though you will find fair-skinned Indians belonging to this community, and in South India you will find dark-skinned Brahmins. But generally my dark skin implied 'Untouchable' or low caste. Sometimes when I was travelling on a bus the conductor would point at me and shout `Coolie!' (`Porter!'), and I was expected to get off the bus and load the roof with luggage. During my second trip to India in 2004, I sometimes experienced people dragging their friends or relatives away from me. It was translated to me that they thought I was either `Untouchable' or a witch doctor who would bring them bad karma. Some people from lower castes thought because I was female, dark and in Western clothing that I must be holy or very rich, and wanted to touch my hands so that they could gain merit, in hope of a better birth next time around.

If I had been born in India, I would have been a financial burden for my family, as the darker you are, the uglier you are considered to be, and some people even believe you are polluted. Although dark-skinned Indian men are able to find women to marry, it is hard for parents to find a husband who will marry their dark-skinned daughter. During a trip to India in 2006 I was told by an Indian friend who is 22 that he was surprised that although my skin was so dark, I still had a pure heart. I was also presented with skin lightener products by shopkeepers when I entered their shops. During this same trip, the small children I spent time living around would often come up and say: "Didi (big sister), what is your father's name?" They were curious about my similar skin colour and different hair, and were trying to work out in their young heads what caste I was from. In India when people hear your last name they will often know what your caste status is, or will be trying to work it out. I often smiled inside when the young girls came to ask questions because I knew that if an African was asking me the same question, they would know instantly I was from slave stock. How else would I have got my double-barrelled English name?

During my second trip, I went on a Buddhist pilgrimage to see the famous sites, and heard about the two Indian heroes of Buddhism since the time of the Buddha. King Ashoka (who lived in the 3rd century BCE) had been so devastated when he realised how many people he had killed while fighting for his kingdom that he declared himself a Buddhist and swore he would never again destroy the lives of human beings. He went around India building Buddhist *stupas* and viharas, and was part of the process of making Buddhism a national religion. However, after his death much was destroyed and Buddhism went into decline.

The second Buddhist hero I heard about is of more recent times. He lived in the 20th century, was born an 'Untouchable' and died a Buddhist. Dr. Bhimrao Ramji Ambedkar brought

Buddhism back to its original soil, reclaiming an indigenous religion. I was so moved by the story of how he committed his whole life to taking the 'Untouchables' out of slavery. He tried to emancipate the whole of India through Buddhism and end the inhumane practices of caste. Through law, politics and religion he set about trying to change the lives of the people of the caste into which he was born. His non-violent fight for the freedom of his people parallels Martin Luther King's fight for the freedom of the African American, or Nelson Mandela's struggle against apartheid. But outside India few people know Ambedkar's name, although, as chairman of the drafting committee of India's Constitution, he was the father of the Indian Republic.

I was also inspired by Dr. Ambedkar's continuous appeal to society that all women should be educated. Believing that if you educated women you educated a nation, he tried to introduce positive discrimination and equal rights for women in the Hindu Code Bill, which he drafted in 1947. While travelling around India, I could see very clearly how women, especially Dalit women, were oppressed because of their caste, living conditions, lack of education, and lack of facilities. At the same time, I was hugely inspired by the Dalit women who had managed to emancipate themselves because of Ambedkar's vision and believed it was their duty to do something for his mission: the emancipation of the Sudras, who are at the bottom of the caste system, born to serve the three castes above them, and the 'Untouchables', who are traditionally not even considered fit to be included in the caste system, but are condemned to be the scavengers of society.

The courageous stories of these women touched me, and I felt stimulated to write about them, and to document the voice of the most oppressed person in India, the Dalit woman, who is oppressed by the Hindu male, the Hindu female and the Dalit male, the woman who is oppressed by her caste, her gender and her religion. To understand the lives of these women, their struggles and their achievements, it is important first to be aware of caste and also to know something more about Dr. Ambedkar, who championed their struggle for basic human rights.

Names and naming are incredibly important and have been the means whereby injustice has been perpetrated through the ages. 'Dalit', 'Down trodden' and Harijans have been used by some sections of Indian society but none of them have met with universal favour. There is no generally accepted solution to this problem. I've decided to use the word 'Untouchable' in the title in inverted commas to highlight to the rest of the world that untouchability despite being outlawed is an ongoing reality throughout India. However I have used the word Dalit in the book to recognise the political campaigns and organisation of people who have fought against the oppression of untouchability.

The Universal Nature of Caste

Caste is a form of slavery that has throughout history systematically organised many races of people in the world, having been used as a system to discriminate between different tribes and races of people living in the same geographical area. Most of the ancient civilisations, including Africa, Greece, Rome and China, used some kind of caste system to determine who is superior and who is inferior. What distinguishes caste in India from that in most other countries is that Indian caste divisions are sanctioned by religion and it's a graded inequality. According to the Rig Veda and other Hindu scriptures, caste is divinely ordained and has a cosmic origin according to the Purush Sukt. This was written as law into the sacred texts and people had no choice but to abide by it, they were forced to accept it. Later on, another caste of people were created. They weren't considered human enough to be designated a caste, and they were considered to be outcastes and polluted in every sense. They were treated less than humans.

Many countries outgrew their caste system as a form of social organisation due to industrialisation. Tribes and races began to assimilate, and people began to follow professions on the basis of skill and talent rather than heredity. Today there are still some places in some countries where caste is used to discriminate between people. But nowhere has it persisted as it has in India, where the whole country has remained divided by caste.

The Indian Caste System

Caste has been the predominant identity of the people of India for thousands of years, and although within the last fifty years significant changes have happened, it is still largely so today. No Hindu is born without a caste, and caste also exists among Indian Christians and Muslims. Every caste member is very conscious of being higher than members of another caste, and no one wants to admit that their caste is lower or more polluted than another. On the positive side, castes does create a sense of identity, solidarity and belonging. Everyone will stick together in their caste: if someone is in trouble, other members of the caste will rally round to help, and many people will try to protect a member of their caste who has committed a crime. This phenomenon is described as "salute above and kick below." One very important feature of caste is endogamy: that is, marriage within one's own caste. In modern/urban India this has created a problem, as people of different castes are meeting in educational institutions, and some people want a 'love marriage' with someone from another caste. However, many parents will refuse to let inter-caste marriages go ahead. Within each caste, there are many sub-castes (*jatis*), each with its own social rules; and the rule is that one should marry someone not just from one's own caste, but from one's own *jati*. The caste system thus divides Indian society into thousands of communities.

Caste rules control all the activities of Hindu men and women: how they dress, what food they eat, what ceremonies they attend. 'Caste permeates every pore of Indian society in hidden, insidious ways. It is so complex; few Indians begin to understand it completely, although it is present in our lives in subtle and not-so-subtle ways. Even though the caste hierarchy is a Hindu construct, conversion does not always help: Buddhists, Christians, Sikhs and Muslims often still cling to their caste identities when searching for marriage partners.'[1]

Caste is such a phenomenon in Indian society that castes are continually dividing and multiplying due to issues of inferiority and superiority within their communities. The writer Edward Luce wrote, 'Indians don't caste a vote, they vote their caste.' Some people claim that even today an Indian takes his caste everywhere he goes. Whether or not this is true, the culture of caste in India may explain why much of the Indian population has not assimilated in the West to the degree that other migrants who have emigrated to Europe or the USA have. As long as caste remains part of Hindu culture, Hindus will not intermarry or have any social intercourse with outsiders.

Caste is handed down from generation to generation, and having been born into a particular caste, you remain in it from birth to death. According to custom, people from different *jatis* do not eat, drink or socialise with each other. The rigidity of the caste system is such that for thousands of years terrible, inhuman atrocities have been acted out on the lowest castes, and these atrocities still happen. Another feature of the caste system (as laid out in an ancient sacred text called the Manusmriti) is that all women are considered to be slaves/outcastes.

The Origin of Caste in India

Many sociologists believe the caste system in India originated as a way of dividing labour, as well as a method of exercising social control and maintaining order. Its power – and almost absolute acceptance – stems from the fact that caste derives religious sanction for India's majority from the 4,000-year-old Manu Sashtra or laws of Manu.[2]

There are many theories of how caste came about in India. Often a person's view of the origin of caste is tied up with their political beliefs, and the theories also change with the times. "Nobody really knows how caste came about. It is a system which has evolved slowly over a long period of time in a culture where there was no systematic chronicling. It seems that India didn't have the same book-keeping as places like China and Europe."[3] One theory is that caste began in India with the migration into the country from the north by the people known as Aryans. Although no one can give an exact date of the Aryan invasion, what we do know is that, after they invaded India, two distinct races, Aryan and non-Aryan, arose, and so inevitably new social groupings emerged. The Aryans brought their own Vedic practices and social groupings which mixed with the existing clan system. They imposed a *varna* system (varna is a Sanskrit word meaning colour/social caste) upon the existing ancient tribal society, and organised the people into endogamous groups.

Though we do not know for certain who was responsible for creating the varna system, we know that it was in existence by the time the Buddhist Pali Canon was written down (around the 1st century BCE), because there are references to it in the Pali scriptures.

'Purusha is described as a primeval giant, not unlike the Norse Ymir, that is sacrificed by the gods (see Purushamedha) and from whose body the world and the varnas (castes) are built. He is described as having a thousand heads and a thousand feet. He emanated Viraj, the female creative principle, from which he is reborn in turn before the world was made out of his parts. In the sacrifice of Purusha, the Vedic chants were first created. The horses and cows were born, the Brahmins were made from Purusha's mouth, the Kshatriyas from his arms, the Vaishyas from his thighs, and the Sudras from his feet. The moon was born from his spirit, the sun from his eyes, the heavens from his skull. Indra and Agni emerged from his mouth.[4]

And we know that it was the Brahmins who were responsible for declaring the division of caste to be divine law.

Manu is a mythical figure variously represented in Hinduism as the progenitor of human beings and the father of all social and moral law. To him is attributed a vast work known as the *Manusmrti*, the 'Laws of Manu', which, among many other aspects of Hindu law, gives divine sanction for the caste system. The text draws upon a passage from the *Rig Veda* which describes how Brahma, the creator god, gave birth to the world.

According to Hindu religious philosophy, Brahma is a Hindu god from whom human evolution began, 'his mouth became the priests (Brahmins), his arms became the warrior (Kshatriyas), his thighs were the merchants (Vaishyas) and from beneath his feet were born the servants (Sudras).

Then there were the outcastes, who were born from outside the body of the creator. They were seen as almost a different species from Brahma's children, and their entry into the divine body was unimaginable. They were outside the social order of the caste system, and consequently excluded from society. This is why they had to live outside the villages and towns: for fear that they would pollute the people who lived there. The work traditionally allotted to them was scavenging, the removal of refuse, and the handling of dead animals and dead bodies.

The Religious Justification for Caste
(Some Citations from the Bhagavad Gita and the Manu Smriti)

The divisions between the many strata of caste were justified by the religious doctrine of karma, which held that one's caste status was determined by one's deeds in a previous life. There was thus no escape from the caste you were born into; the idea was that if you fulfilled the duties of your caste faithfully, that would ensure a favourable rebirth. It was those at the top of the caste hierarchy, the Brahmins, who – according to the caste system itself – were responsible, as priests and teachers of the people, for preserving the scriptures which sanctified the system and, by giving it divine authority, placed it beyond question for thousands of years. It was also the Brahmins who performed all the rites, rituals and ceremonies. They developed a secretive priestcraft by means of which they were able to keep their privileged status. Priesthood was handed down from father to son, and they "devised an ingenious method"[5] to maintain their position. "Religion was brought in. They propounded a theory of creation which placed the class system on a permanent basis. Thus the class system was converted to the caste system. With a religious dogma as its basis the caste system came to assume religious significance. Now, whatever was associated with the name of religion was regarded as sacred."[6]

The Brahmins were the only ones who could teach the scriptures, and to the Kshatriyas and the Vaishyas was given the privilege of being taught. But the Sudras, the outcastes, and women from all varnas were denied access to the scriptures. It was none of their business; they were born to serve the Brahmins and the higher castes. They were born, in other words, into slavery. The Sudras' life was slightly better than that of the outcastes because at least they were allowed to live in the villages, but they did all the menial jobs like labouring and farm work for the three castes above them. The outcastes had to do the scavenging and filthiest work for all four *varnas*. "The outcastes, the Tribals and the Sudras, who have all been used as slaves, account for almost 80 per cent of the population. India is the only country in the world where the majority of the population has been used as slaves. The slavery of India was much worse than that of the Negroes in America and Europe, because in India we were not only physically, mentally and economically enslaved; we were also religiously, educationally, culturally enslaved."[7]

The Brahmins were responsible for devising rigid and degrading ways of treating the outcastes, known more recently as 'Untouchables'. "In Poona, the capital of the Peshwa, the untouchable was required to carry, strung from his waist, a broom to sweep away from behind the dust he trod on lest a Hindu walking on the same should be polluted. In Poona the untouchable was required to carry an earthen pot, hung around his neck wherever he went, for holding his spit lest a spit falling on earth should pollute a Hindu who might unknowingly happen to tread on it."[8]

Changes in the Twentieth Century

In the early 20th century the Brahmins tried to bring all four *varnas*, along with the outcastes, together under one national identity: Hinduism. This phenomena is known as the Hinduisation. Although the Vedic religion had existed for thousands of years, the term Hindu is a political term which first appeared in the early 1900s. The elite Indians, the majority of whom were Brahmins, realised that if they were to keep their power they needed to create a national identity which would bring together all the castes of India. They took a term which had been given to the whole of India hundreds of years ago, when the Indians were described by Chinese travellers as 'the people of the Indus river'; the Muslims, who came later, also used this description. "Since the Brahmins were a minority in India they would not be able to have a political identity based on Brahminism alone. They could see this would not help them to rule India, because they would be cut off from the rest of the populace as a minority, so they needed a national identity. Hence in 1917 came the terms Hindu, Hindi and Hindustan. At that time the first Hindu nationalist party was formed."[9]

In this same period, those outside the caste system were given a legal identity for the first time. The British colonial census of 1911 grouped together all the communities who were called 'polluted' and referred to them as 'untouchable'; this was the first time that term was used. The British then named them the Scheduled Castes, 'scheduled' because they were listed on a schedule appended to the Constitution of British India, in the Government of India Act 1919, which gave the outcastes of India their first legal identity. Scheduled Castes became the official legal term in 1936.

The ex 'Untouchables' have been called a multitude of names, from 'Chandala' used in the *Manausmriti*, '*Avarna*', outside the four *varna* system to 'Depressed Classes' used by British officials to Mahatma Gandhi naming them '*Harijans*', 'children of God'. Many people felt that this was an equivalent of 'Uncle Tom', perceiving it as a paternalistic and patronising categorisation of a group condemned to remain in slavery. Dalit leader Bhaurao, Gaikwad said in reference to this term in 1935: "It is no use only giving Untouchables a sweet name, something practical should be done to ameliorate their conditions."[10] The commonly used term today is Dalit, a Sanskrit word which means 'divided, broken'. It has become a political term which refers to broken or ground-down people, distressed, crushed or downtrodden. Many people from this community see the name Dalit as a term of assertion owing to its shock value. It was first used by the 19th century social revolutionist Jatirao Phule, and its usage was popularised by the Dalit Panthers, a political group that was founded in 1972.

"Today the name Dalit has united all people of various segments (deemed Untouchable and severely oppressed with religious legitimation) together... Although these groups have different cultures, they are all united under one banner – Dalit."[11]

In more recent times both academics and the Indian media continue to popularise the usage of Dalit. Dalits today include those castes which are the most oppressed in India, the Scheduled Castes and Scheduled Tribes. But although Dalit is the most often used contemporary term, there are still many people who do not like to define themselves as 'Dalit', especially if they have converted to Islam, Christianity or Buddhism. And there are those who prefer to call themselves Ambedkarites to demonstrate their faith in his teachings.

Then there is the fourth varna, the Sudras, who are called the Other Backward Classes, (OBCs), and they also suffer much discrimination. And some of these have won the fight to be classified as Scheduled Tribes, which empowers them to have the same reservation rights as Dalits. Ambedkar dedicated much of his writing trying to explain who were the Sudras and why they were so oppressed. The irony today is that it is claimed that most crimes against the Dalit community are by the OBC community. For example, where the OBCs are landholders, the landless Dalits are their labourers. In the South, the landowning Thevars are OBCs and have been known to murder the Puraiyans who are Dalit.

And so, since Ambedkar's death, it seems the gap between many OBCs and Dalits has become hostile and huge. Despite the fact that there are some OBCs who have fought the government to be classified as Scheduled Tribes or Scheduled Castes so that they can have access to the special reservations.

Ironically, some higher castes Hindus argue that the divide between them and the Dalit is minimal today, as some upper castes have changed tactics and are cooperating more with the Dalit and OBC communities. Mayawati's (Leader, Bahujan Samaj Party and Chief Minister of the State of Uttar Pradesh) main advisor is a Brahmin and he put together an alliance of upper castes, Muslims, and Dalits to beat the right wing BJP Party.

Ambedkar would have been greatly saddened by the conflicts between the OBCs and Dalits, but elated with the

Bahujan Samaj Party; it was his dream to have a party bringing different castes together to fight casteism. He saw this as part of the way to ending casteism.

When thinking of India's history in the 20th century, most people outside India will call to mind Mahatma Gandhi, who was a caste Hindu (merchant caste) who wanted to see an end to 'Untouchability'. He once wrote to the British government and said: "I feel that no penance that Hindus may do can in any way compensate for the calculated degradation to which they have consigned the depressed classes for centuries." Gandhi believed that two conditions were needed if India was to have true independence: the abolition of 'Untouchability', and unity between Muslims and Hindus. However, he believed that the four-varna system appropriately defined the duties of people in society. In his view all duties, whether those of priests or scavengers, had equal status and carried equal merit before the gods. Instead of eradicating caste he therefore tried to create a fifth *varna*, *Panchama*, for the people he called Harijans. He didn't succeed; the name Harijans was used until the 1980s, but Harijans were still treated as 'Untouchable', they were still considered to be outside the *varna* system.

Many people would say that it was not Gandhi but Bhimrao Ramji Ambedkar who was the true saviour of the 'Untouchables'. He himself was born an 'Untouchable' of the *Mahar* caste, but he became the most highly educated Indian person of his time, and is recognised by many as the inspiration for the uplift of the 'Untouchable' community, having led a major non-violent revolt against Brahminism.

The first fundamental difference between Gandhi and Ambedkar was caste. Gandhi was born into the merchant caste, into wealth and privilege; Ambedkar was born into the 'Untouchable' caste, poverty and oppression. Secondly, Gandhi believed that India's problems stemmed from British imperialism and the degradation of the village system. Gandhi wanted to keep the caste system while trying to get rid of 'Untouchability'. But Ambedkar believed that neither British imperialism nor the degradation of the village was really the issue, instead believing that the crux of the problem, the mother of all problems in India, was caste. He said that unless you got rid of caste, there could be no social, economic or cultural transformation.

Ambedkar's whole life was about fighting for the emancipation of Indian society. He educated himself in the hope that this would be enough for him to be treated equally in his country, but he discovered that he was still subject to caste discrimination, despite all his scholarly distinction. As a lawyer he was able to win some important cases for his community, but that still didn't bring about the kind of change he could see was necessary. Then he entered politics and, through his appointment as chairman of the Indian Constitution committee, changed the face of the whole Indian nation, creating a democratic society for every Indian person to live in. But this was still not enough to give equality to women and the lower classes in India. So, in the end, he publicly denied the Hindu religion and became a Buddhist. He made a resolution at the famous Yeola Conference in 1935: "Even though I was born in the Hindu religion, I will not die in the Hindu religion." He saw leaving Hinduism as the only way out of caste oppression for himself and his community. But it was twenty years before he took the step of converting to Buddhism, after considering many other religions, philosophies and systems of thought. He wanted the 'Untouchables' to throw out their Hindu gods and embrace Buddhism, because, in his view, Buddhism offered the best possibility of ending casteism.

"With his breadth of economic and cultural analysis, Ambedkar should have stood in the forefront of the men whose ideas shaped India. Yet he is barely admitted into their ranks. With the failure of a broad political alliance, in spite of his many writings and policies on crucial issues of the time, from the question of Pakistan to that of the economic structuring of independent India, Ambedkar has retained a place in the collective memory of India primarily as the leader of India's Untouchables."[12] In his campaign to free India from casteism, Dr. Ambedkar should be named one of the great sons of India. He is not just the hero of the Dalit community, not just the hero of equal rights for women. He is one of the heroes of the Indian nation, who left a blueprint from which many generations of Indian people will benefit. Many Christians, Muslims and Dalits in positions of responsibility or high-status professions would acknowledge that this is because of Ambedkar's insight, because it was he who implemented reservations (positive discrimination) for the minorities in India within the Constitution.

Many women, caste Hindus or not, would have to admit the same. It is true that some of these people are in places of influence in their own right, not because of reservations. But all these communities have benefited greatly. If Ambedkar had lived long enough, perhaps the whole of India might have converted to Buddhism, a religion which he believed would eradicate caste and bring about the equality of all individuals in the Indian nation.

The Situation Today

Caste discrimination was made illegal in 1950, and the movement begun by Dr. Ambedkar has made progress in various ways. But caste is still very much part of Indian life today; and caste discrimination is still powerful too, although it is technically against the law. When a low caste person claims their dignity through education, by improving their status through acquiring land or achieving influence in society, this poses a threat to the caste system. High caste Hindus, indignant that a low caste person should move above their station in life, as they see it, continue to oppress such social mobility through harassment, burning property, raping women and sometimes committing murder. It has been estimated that in India today one in every 25 people suffers caste discrimination on the basis of their work, their blood line or their religion. A website called Combating Caste states that every two hours a Dalit is assaulted, and every day three Dalit women are raped, two Dalits are murdered and two Dalit houses are burned. In 2005 'New Internationalist' reported that an estimated 25-60 million people in India are bonded labourers, working in slave-like conditions in order to pay off a debt, and the majority of them are Dalits. In September 2006, in the State of Maharashtra, it was reported that four members of a Dalit family were tortured, gang-raped, humiliated and murdered because of their caste. They were second generation Buddhists who had refused to give in to the demands of caste Hindus and had come forward as witnesses against caste Hindus. This crime has agitated much rioting in the State of Maharashtra in reaction to what people saw as a lack of response from the government.

Crimes like this are part of the everyday life of the Dalit community; and the people who are oppressing them are the very people to whom they have to go for help if they want justice. Indian society can be so corrupt that a bribe made to a high caste Hindu in a position of power will in many cases cause him to succumb and not follow up Dalit complaints. Often caste solidarity will be enough. Despite legislation against 'Untouchability', many crimes against Dalits are not brought to court, and perpetrators are rarely punished. It is claimed that in states like Rajasthan the judges will not go ahead with court procedures for any crime against a Dalit unless there is a non-Scheduled Caste witness willing to give evidence. Older and younger generations of the Dalit community tell the same stories of 'Untouchability' and discrimination. Casteism in India is a human rights crime which has gone mostly unchallenged by the rest of the world.

Although since the 1980s there has been real evidence of empowerment among the Dalit communities, with Dalits in the federal government as ministers, currently the post of Chief Minister of Maharashtra (2007) has been filled by a Dalit, Shinde, and the Bahujan Samaj Party socially and politically mobilising the Dalits, and with their dramatic election win in Uttar Pradesh 2007, with a clear majority. And Mayawati from the Jatav/Chamar caste who has become its Chief Minister for the fourth time, the majority of the Dalit community still remain oppressed.

Figures from *Untouchability in Rural India 2006* highlight the following:

* Public health workers refused to visit Dalit homes in 33 per cent of villages.

* Dalits were prevented from entering police stations in 27.6 per cent of villages.

* Dalit children had to sit separately while eating in 37.8 per cent of government schools.

* Dalits didn't get mail delivered to their homes in 23.5 per cent of villages.

* Dalits were denied access to water sources in 48.4 per cent of villages because of segregation and untouchabilty practices.

* Literacy rates for Dalit women are as low as 37.8 per cent in rural India.

Women's Voices

India still oppresses its women; many are still the outcastes of society. In uneducated communities, girl children are a burden, and in rural areas some are even burned to death as soon as they are born. If a girl survives her birth she is all too often considered to be the lowest of the low. The Dalit women are the least educated women in society, and it is they who are the worst victims of Indian society; their caste and their gender relegate them to a life of inequality. Many Dalit women are victims of domestic violence from their husbands. After a long day at work labouring or in the fields, the men drink and come home and beat their wives. In the fields where the women work, if they argue about their rate of pay they are often beaten and raped by their high caste employers, who are sometimes encouraged to do this by their wives. A woman's husband may work in the same field and do the same work for the same hours, but her employer will pay her less because she is a woman. There have been incidents where a Dalit woman's husband has owned land and high caste people have demanded ownership. When her husband refuses to give it up, its his wife who suffers, gang-raped by high caste Hindu men in retaliation. The Dalit woman has no status; she is at the bottom of the heap in Indian society. And in the Hindu scriptures all women are considered Sudras (slaves, menials to serve the higher caste people) irrespective of their caste background.

The voices heard in this book range from those of the ex 'Untouchable' women who converted to Buddhism in 1956, to their daughters who were born Buddhist, to women who call themselves Ambedkarites because of Ambedkar's philosophy, to Dalit women who were born Hindu and have converted to Buddhism in recent years, to those who are still Hindu and belong to the Scheduled Castes and Scheduled Tribes, and a few women from the Backward Classes who have been classified as Dalit, and align themselves with the Dalit struggle. The voices are mainly from the State of Maharashtra, as this is where the initial conversion happened, but other voices from outside the State of Maharashtra are represented, and many of them say that 'Untouchability' is still a major feature of their lives today. Most of these women have told their stories anonymously because to reveal their identity might put their lives at risk. I have kept to the integrity of the women's voices as much as possible, so that the reader can read and hear the voices on the pages speaking in Indian English. These interviews took place from September 2006 to January 2007. Their stories are a slice of life in India's complex society today.

Snapshots from the Past

Victims of the past
Lived in, worn memories
The past has now gone

I am between 70 and 75 – I don't know exactly because my birth date was never recorded. I came from a village near Satara in Maharashtra, where I was treated as 'Untouchable'. As a young girl I had to walk with my hands behind my back, holding a broom so that when I walked my footsteps were wiped out and the Brahmins would not be polluted by them. Some of the other 'Untouchables' in the village had their brooms strapped to their backs, to trail behind them as they walked. Whenever our shadow fell upon a Brahmin, they would run with fear and sprinkle water over us, because they thought that if they stepped into our shadow they would be polluted. The only time we were allowed near the Brahmins' houses was when one of their animals died, and then we would have to drag it away.

I remember having to run from village to village, informing the people that a Brahmin had died. I could run all day and not be given any food or water, because the Brahmins were too scared to come near me. If I was lucky I would cup my hands and they would throw dirty water at me to drink. They would never give me a cup to drink from. This was the situation at the time. We had to beg for our water and food, and if we were lucky they gave us the stale remains of their meals. When we worked for them we were only paid in food, and what we got depended on how they were feeling. Sometimes we went without food entirely.

But now the situation has changed. Many of my people have moved to the cities, where it is very different. I was fortunate that I heard about Dr. Ambedkar in the 1950s. I attended several of his lectures and was present at the *deeksha* (conversion) to Buddhism fifty years ago. My whole family, including my in-laws, attended the programme, and my husband was an active leader in his movement.

Dr. Ambedkar has been so important in my life because he didn't believe in casteism, and made no distinction between people. He is the only person in this country that has done so much for my people.

I have never heard of Dr. Ambedkar and he never came to my village. I'm happy being a Hindu. What is the use of being angry about the past? That is just how it was in those days. I believe that we should never speak ill of others or do ill to others. We should treat each other kindly.

I was born 70 years ago into the Matang caste, a Scheduled Caste, in the State of Maharashtra. My family were the only *Matangs* among the high caste Hindus (they were all Marathas) in a village in Amravati. There had been many more members of my family in this village, but many had died from causes I was never told about, and we were the last Matang family to survive.

Everyone in the village believed in the gods, but I never knew who they were or why we worshipped them. I just knew that if we prayed to them they could help us. I didn't go to school, and neither did my three sisters. We were brought up in a family of labourers, so we were expected to help in the fields, or stay at home with our mother and help collect wood, clean and cook. We never went out in the village very much because we were not allowed to be near the Maratha people unless we were working. They were afraid of us touching them. We earned money from making brooms to sweep the temples in our village, but we were never allowed to go inside them. We made brooms for the Maratha houses too, but they never let us go anywhere near their houses. When my sisters and I delivered the brooms, we had to stand a long way away and put them down, and the Maratha people would come out and throw water at us, so that dust from our feet didn't pollute the outside of their homes.

When I was fourteen I married, and soon after that my whole family left this village and moved to a slum village on the outskirts of a city. This was very different as we were all from the same caste, which meant we could mingle easily with everyone. I've never met another Brahmin or Maratha since.

Since *deeksha* (conversion) my family has not had to suffer 'Untouchability'. But before this my family and many other people suffered at the hands of the Brahmins and other high caste Hindus. I'm in my 70s, and I experienced severe 'Untouchability' for at least the first 29 years of my life. In my village, the *Mahars* from the Untouchable caste had to wait for their food. We were never fed before the Brahmins or other high caste people. If we stood outside their shops and ordered a drink, our drinks were served in broken cups. As a child, I was never allowed to sit near one of them, never allowed to touch one of them, or play with them.

I used to collect cow dung and make it into patties so that they could have fuel for their fires. We were never given any for our homes. If we didn't turn up to work on time they would beat us. If we complained they starved us, or only gave us the meat of their dead animals which had died from disease.

Of course my people got very angry – we were treated worse than dogs – but we were totally dependent on the Brahmins and the high caste Hindus for our food, our livelihood. There was nothing we could do. Every time one of them walked by us, we had to fall to their feet and treat them with respect.

The Present

Evicted from our land
High caste Hindus burn house down
Human Rights issue

I live in a Hindu village where 'Untouchability' still happens. I'm only 18 so I'm not talking about the distant past. In fact I can't give you the name of my village through fear of persecution, but I want to tell this story for my family and all the other low caste people who have suffered.

The name of my village is my last name. Where I'm from, the name of your village is always your last name, and this will give your caste away. This means that when I go for a job in my district, people immediately know what caste I'm from and will not employ me. I am extremely fortunate not to be married, because in the Hindu culture most girls from low caste families are married at 12. I've had a lot of pressure put on me to marry, but I've managed to avoid it because of my brother, who works for the social movement and has fought against my family about this. He has seen two sisters suffer. One sister married a man with no money and my family have to send food to her home every week so they can eat.

Many of my friends from my village married at the age of ten, and some of them have been tortured in their marriages because their parents couldn't pay the dowry. My people are poor. Some days we have food to eat, and some days we don't, it depends on whether the high caste people feel like paying us properly for our work. All the land around here is owned by one high caste family, and so we have to rely on this family and their relatives for our wages. If you fall out with any member of this family you will suffer.

My grandfather managed to get some land, but a member of the high caste family seized it, and he was thrown out and all his livestock was taken. Fortunately my grandfather found a document that said he owned the land, so he put up a legal fight and won. As a result, my family have been persecuted by the high caste people, and they continue to seek revenge. They have stolen goats from my grandfather and have tried to destroy his land.

My elder sister recently married a man from a very poor village. From the dowry my parents paid, her husband built a small house on the outskirts of our village. The high caste family noticed this new house and were furious. They knew it belonged to a low caste person because it was on the perimeter of the village, and they soon found out that it belonged to my family. One evening, members of the ruling family arrived in the middle of the night and started demanding that my community give them alcohol. We refused to give them any as they were already very drunk, so they began to beat people up. My sister stepped out of her house and argued with some of them. They mocked her and then torched her house. Luckily nobody was inside.

We reported this crime to the police, but nothing happened because the police are all related to the high caste family. My brother, who works for a human rights organisation, was furious. He said that he wouldn't let these people get away with it and took the matter up. This led to three members of the ruling family being arrested. However, the high caste family mounted a big campaign. First they threatened all the witnesses who came forward and told them to withdraw or watch their backs. Then they managed to hunt down my brother and told him if he didn't drop the case they would kill him. My brother didn't care. He said: "If they want to kill me, they can go ahead. This is my family we are talking about." My mother broke down and begged him to drop it, but he wouldn't. So they continued to threaten my family, and my parents wouldn't let any of us out of the house for fear that we would be kidnapped.

The village council, which is controlled by the ruling family, called a meeting which all of us attended, including my brother. I was sitting beside him and I saw how one of the high caste people took his hand strongly, shook it, and said into his ear: "We will kill you." My brother smiled, but I was very frightened. At this meeting my brother said firmly that he was going ahead with the case. However, no witnesses from the low caste people came forward, and the high caste people managed to put the blame for burning the house onto eight members of my family. My mother was hysterical when we got home and begged my brother to stop. She warned him that he would get no support from his family. He looked at my mother and father and said: "OK, I will drop the case, but don't tell me again if anything happens to this family. I am not interested." And he walked out. We knew that he had dropped the case because three days later the three men who were arrested were back in the village causing trouble.

My parents sent me away soon after this; they were afraid I would be attacked. I was sent to a house in the hope of marriage. But because I am close to my brother, he has continued to support me. He has found a college for me to attend where I can learn about social work for one whole year. It's in Nagpur and it is called Nagaloka. It's a school for Dalit people of different backgrounds. This has given me an opportunity to feel solidarity with my community. But I am still worried about my family back home, as I know that the discrimination still continues.

Mayor of Pune
Today - Caste does not happen
The Congress Party

I was born into a large family 37 years ago. I was educated in a government school up to the 7th standard, when I was about 12 years old. My father owned a shop during my childhood but in my adolescence he became an active political leader. This had a huge impact on my life. When I was about 28 my father inspired me to run for a local election to be a corporater (councillor). There was a reserve for a woman to be a corporater of a ward in Pune. There are 191 corporaters in Pune, and I managed to become one of them. Thirty-three per cent of us are from the Dalit community and 64 per cent of us are women. I was elected because of my father's good work, but I proved myself and was elected to serve a second term. Then in 2003 I became Mayor of Pune, the second largest city in the State of Maharashtra.

Since I've become Mayor, I have been working to try and create a better city for the people. I have created a beautiful Japanese garden for the local people to visit. I've introduced a sewage treatment plan to help create better drainage in the city. I've also been working on developing the slums. Forty-two per cent of Pune's population live in slums, and they are 99 per cent filled with Dalit people. This is because most of the people living in the slums have migrated from the villages in the hope of finding work and educating their children. In the city they know they can get free education and more opportunities to earn money. There are so many people in the slums because they are poor. They come from generations of poor people. In the slums and the villages I have set up self-help groups for the women so they can learn how to bank and look after their money.

It is my vision to give people in these areas good houses. I have introduced a government scheme called Slum Rehabilitation

Authority, or SRA, to help the Dalit community. I believe in developing the slums. When I first became Mayor, I was offered mayoral quarters and refused them. Later Sonia Gandhi, the leader of the Congress Party, offered me a house. I said: "No. I was born in the slums, I live in the slums, and I will go to work from the slums." My husband is not in a government job. He works on the railways. I'm very happy in my marriage and enjoy the life I live. I am developing the area I live in rather than moving away from it.

All the people in the Congress Party are supporting me to do my work. I have full support as a woman; they do not think that I am from the Dalit caste or that I am a woman. I have the people behind me. My father and Dr. Ambedkar have been the inspiration which has enabled me to work effectively for the people of Pune. Ambedkar is like a god to me; because of him I am sitting in this chair, because of him I am Mayor. My father also encouraged me and recognised my potential. Nowadays caste is not happening in India. The people are all together now. It's not how it used to be. In the Congress Party we all work together.

Outcastes

Fourth born is cursed
Baby girl outcaste from birth
Dumped with the gods

The story of my childhood is a typical Hindu story, typical of many young girls in India. I may be 30, but what I am going to tell you I assure you still happens commonly today in villages like the one where I grew up.

Like most men in India, my father expected a baby boy, but when the first child was born it was a girl. Like most men, my father was disappointed, but he managed to get over it, because he had a good job with a decent wage, and so he knew he could afford his daughter's dowry. My mother had two more girls, and after the third I'm told that my father said: "Go to your brother's home, and if you have a boy, you can come back to this house." I was the fourth baby, and – as you see – I was a girl. This was traumatic for my mother but she still returned with me in her arms. But my father threw her out and refused to love me.

My father's sister-in-law pitied my mother and managed to talk to my father. He took her back but refused to take me. My sister-in-law persisted and told my mother she couldn't abandon me. But when I was taken back into the family, I was ignored. I became the outcaste of the family. My three elder sisters were treated differently. When my father came home from work he only had love for them. They would run towards him and he would pick them up. If I ran towards him he would turn and walk away. I know that if my father had loved me, my mother, like most Indian women, would have done the same, because they just copy and accept whatever their husbands do. After I was born another daughter came, but it was different for her because in Hindu superstition it is believed that if you have five daughters a boy will definitely come. And this proved to be right, because the sixth child was a boy, and so my fifth sister was very lucky indeed.

My life in this family was terrible. My father blamed me for whatever went wrong. I was blamed for all the bad *karma* in their lives, blamed for them all being born *Mahars*. I was given the job of a scavenger. It was my duty to bring cow dung to the house and squash it onto the walls for insulation, and make round patties for fuel. I was the 'Untouchable' of my family. We were all ex 'Untouchables', living on the edge of the village, but they made me do all the shit work.

When I was five, my job was to bring coal from the railway before school. One day I was late picking up the coal and there was no more to be found. I panicked and worried about what my family would do, and then I turned and saw a few pieces of coal lying on the ground. A caste Hindu child saw it at the same moment, and as I went to pick it up, he screamed: "No, you're a *Mahar*; you can't have it." I ignored him and picked it up because I was there first and knew what would happen if I went home empty-handed. He climbed up a pole by the railway lines, and while I was gathering the coal, he dropped a huge rock on my head, splitting it open. Someone in the village found me lying in my blood and took me home, but my father was furious. All he was concerned about was how much the medical charges would be. My mother begged him to do something, but he called her names like prostitute, and she had no choice but to try and heal my wound herself.

My sisters were also cruel to me. I had to collect all the water from the well for my family. Every day I had to cross a big sewage ditch. One day when I was eight I decided to wear my sister's sandals as my father refused to buy me new shoes. But as I crossed the ditch, one of the sandals fell into the sewage, and I couldn't get it out. When I returned my sister took me back to the sewage and forced me into the dirty water. As I stood up, I could feel the leeches on my back, which were itching very much. But my sister stood over me and said: "You must find my sandal." The leeches were sucking my blood and I didn't know what to do. I had to go home crying with them on my back. My mother tried tweezers but in the end she had to apply a lot of salt to get rid of them. She felt sorry for me and went to see if she could find the sandal. My sister left me alone after it was found, but they all still continued to bully me.

When I was nine, I tried to run away, because my family said I was a curse and refused to feed me properly. I began living outside, eating fruit like guavas and mangoes. I wandered around without clothes. I slept on the railway with other children like me and lived off banana skins till one day when a neighbour found me sleeping naked by the railway lines. He wrapped clothing around me and took me back to my family home, and he said to my father: "You are careless. Why is your child living like this? You must take care of her." My father was frightened and from that day he was different. He did feed me, but still kept reminding me I was the total outcaste of the family because I was born the fourth girl. He still beat me, but it was bearable to live at home.

I returned to school and continued with all the chores. But when I was ten, I failed my school exams, so my father said: "Right, there is nothing else for you in this home." My neighbour could see what was happening and invited me to live with him and his wife. They allowed me to retake my exams and continue with school, but I had to go out and work for them in return. I began picking up coal from the railway line and selling it. My father was furious when he found out; he said it was bringing shame on his name. I decided to run away again and look after myself.

I managed to make a little money through selling anything I could scavenge, and I went to the second school in the village. I lived with another family who didn't have children and they looked after me well. Although I had very little time to study because of having to work to earn my keep, I listened to the teachers carefully, and when I was 16, I successfully passed the 10th standard exam. I decided I wanted to go to college outside the village, but I was so poor I wasn't able to continue straightaway. I returned to my family and my mother was pleased with me. But when I wanted to apply for college, I couldn't find my caste certificate, which I needed to get my scholarship. My eldest sister had stolen it. I wasn't frightened of her any more and punched her, and we got into a terrible fight. My father heard us, and he pulled me away and started beating me. But from nowhere I found my strength. I took a knife to him and said: "If you touch me again, I will chop your body into pieces, otherwise I would rather die." I warned him that I meant every word. He walked away from me and I left my home.

I managed to get my certificate back. On my first day at college, I turned up with no shoes and torn clothes and people laughed at me. I couldn't cope with this teasing, so I left and went out to work. My family had strong Hindu practices and I was very much influenced by them. While building roads, I became quite sick and was taken to the hospital. My father collected me because he didn't want to pay the bill, and took me to a Hindu Baba (saint). This Baba took care of me and gave me food. Many people came to worship him daily, but I became sicker. One day he tried to rape me. I knew this was wrong, and with my last bit of strength I managed to leave with some of his followers. I was unable to walk or even go to the toilet properly, but they kindly took me to a woman who was a sacred living goddess. She gave me ash to eat and this medicine cured me completely of all my ailments. Her name was Sati Anusaya Maya.

Sati Maya was an inspiration for me because she cured me, and I felt strong again and saw that I could be an independent woman. She had many worshippers who came daily to give her food and money. She lived naked in the woods, and when her disciples came they would wash her. They would splash water over her body and try to catch the water falling from her breasts and drink it, because they believed it would give them good karma. We all believed it would benefit us in our lives. On festival days when we celebrated her, we played the drums at full moon, and prepared garlands to put around her neck. We spread candles all around her, and offered her many fruits and other food. And we sang many songs for her, and did three pujas a day to celebrate her. The spirit of Sati Maya would enter our bodies and we would become breathless and chant uncontrollably, and fall to the ground exhausted.

I know it sounds ridiculous, but this is Hindu culture. I spent much of my childhood in my next door neighbour's house worshipping the gods and goddesses, and praying to them. So it was natural for me to follow this goddess when I was in great need. I loved her and she cared for me. I was the only one who lived with her. I got to eat all the wonderful food that people left, and wear all the beautiful clothes. It was the first time somebody took proper care of me, and she cured all my diseases. I lived with her and worshipped her for almost nine years till I was about 25. Then she began to change slightly and started acting strangely towards her disciples. She would be quite aggressive to them when they came to leave gifts, and I began to worry. It made me look at my life, and I realised I had no job. What would I do if she died? She didn't want me to leave, so I ran away in the middle of the night.

It was hard, and I felt lost, but I found a job straightaway. The first big factory I came across when I entered a nearby city offered me a sweeping job, and I earned enough money to rent a room in a slum. All of a sudden I went from extreme poverty to earning the kind of money I had never seen before. I began to think about marriage and a home of my own. I fell in love with a man but he was married. I thought about returning to Sati Maya but I knew that would not be right. In desperation I sent a card to a friend I had met while living with Sati Maya, and she wrote back and told me about the *Dhamma* and Dr. Ambedkar and how it was time to give up my goddess worship. I didn't quite understand, but her words filled me with joy. Just before Diwali, she sent me another card and told me about a Buddhist retreat, and I have never looked back since. I committed myself to the work of Ambedkar and the Buddhist path a year later.

Through this journey of mine I have learned to accept my family conditioning. Of course I feel angry sometimes, and think that if they hadn't followed all the superstitions and discrimination of Indian culture my life would have been different. But I would have still been a *Mahar* in a Hindu village being oppressed by all the casteism, as my brother's and sisters' families are. They live in villages where they have to endure a lot of prejudice for being the caste they are. All my sisters married young and are duty bound to their husbands and in-laws. But my family have disowned me so I don't have to get married. Because of the way I grew up, I was led to the *Dhamma* and Dr. Ambedkar. Because of my family, I could begin to change my life. I am grateful for that. I am living an independent life as a single woman, with much joy in my heart, and it gives me pleasure to help other women like me. I work in a non-government organisation helping Dalit women of all religions and castes to set up businesses so that they can have independence from male society.

Female with polio
I'm a financial burden
Begging is my life

I am illiterate because I have polio. I was born in a village where there were no schools nearby, and I was unable to walk the one-hour journey to school and the one-hour journey back. My parents were Dalit labourers. They had five girls and two boys, so educating me was not a priority. I've never been to school in my life. Instead, I had to stay at home and help with the domestic work. I hated going out to play because the children would throw stones at me and make fun of me, and I hated being at home because my brothers and sisters were never kind to me. They often teased me or ignored me, and left me out of their games. My parents were always very kind to me, but they didn't know what to do when I ran crying to them. I wasn't happy at all as a child, and didn't understand why I was different. I knew one side of my body could hardly move, but I wanted to be like everybody else.

When my eldest brother married, I was sent off to live with him and his wife. There was no hope of finding me a husband. I was about ten years old and didn't want to go, but I had no choice. His wife treated me like a slave. She wanted me to do all the work in the house and would often beat me. After a year of torture, I decided to run away. I managed to get a ride to the nearest train station in Hyderabad, took the express train, and ended up in Pune.

I arrived at Pune station with no money and didn't know what to do, so I just sat on the platform for two weeks and watched the trains go by. Sometimes people gave me food and tea, and sometimes men would come up to me and try to touch me. Because I was very young the men would tease me. Then one day after two weeks of sleeping, eating and living on the platform, a kind man crawled up to me and asked if I needed help. He was much older than me and had polio in all the lower parts of his body. After taking care of me for the day and giving me food to eat, he said: "I am living alone, will you come and live with me?" I didn't know what else to do. I had no money to go back home, and I didn't want to see my sister-in-law again. So I said "Yes."

He had very little money as he was a beggar on the train station, so I tried to get domestic work, but nobody would employ me. I remembered my 15 days of sitting on the platform and people giving me things, so I realised I could beg too. I was 12 years old when I began begging, and it was very hard to begin with. There were many beggars, and many of them were young girls like me. Some looked like boys with their hair cut short, and they even spoke like boys. They were all very strong and gathered in gangs with the boys. I wasn't able to join them because of my polio, but they were always kind to me. I think most of us were from the Dalit community, though I can't be absolutely certain. But most of us had run away from poverty, domestic violence or sexual abuse. There were many people like me with polio, and many who had other diseases too, and others had migrated from the villages and couldn't find work. We were all friendly with each other and supported each other in our work.

I soon learned that it was better to go to the high class areas to beg, so I began travelling to MG Road. I would put a scarf over my head, sit down on the floor with my crutches beside me, and put my hand out to beg. I still do this today. Some people are really kind, while others shout insults at me and spit at me. Some men want me as their prostitute. But my husband gets worse treatment than me because he is a man. Sometimes the shops call the police and we are arrested, taken away to jail, and have to pay Rs. 500 ($12) to avoid being in prison for one year. On a good day, I can earn as much as Rs. 40, but on a bad day, I earn nothing.

After three years of living like this, I became pregnant with my first child. I had to continue to beg because we didn't have enough money to support us. Also, my husband often drinks away his money, and comes home with no money for me. If I complain, he beats me. So I try to earn enough money for both of us. After our second child, I found out why my husband had not married me. One day his first wife turned up with his two children. She has no polio, but demanded that we give her money. Since then we have had to earn money for her family as well as ours. I asked my husband why he didn't tell me, but he just answered that if he had, I would not have come home to live with him.

Because I am so poor, a friendly doctor working in the slum that I live in suggested I send my children to a hostel where they could get free education. My daughter and son now live at a Christian hostel, and all their food, board and education is paid for by the priests. This is helpful, because now I only have to worry about feeding them during the holidays. My children are seven and eight now and have started to feel ashamed of what I do. When they come back home for the holidays they say: "Don't go begging any more. We are grown up now and people laugh at us, and we feel ashamed." I tell them angrily: "Your father and I are not able to do any other work. Don't torture your parents like this." They don't understand that because of our polio we are shunned. The people in the slum we live in know that we do this work and never say anything unkind to our faces. I do feel angry that I have to beg, especially after a day of earning nothing, and then I have to come home and cook and clean for my husband. If I could, I would do domestic work for other people. But they won't let me because they think I'm 'Untouchable' and that they will catch my disease.

I want my children to be educated so that they can see what we have to do, and so that they can get a proper job. I know that because they are from the Dalit community it may be hard for them to get work. I am grateful for their free education, as I can only make enough money to feed two mouths. My home is very basic, just one room with a bathroom, and a few things inside. I'm not always able to keep up with my payments to my husband's first family.

I have been home to visit my family, but my father has died, so I only see my mother. When I told her what I did to earn money she cried and pleaded with me to stop, and asked why I have to do such things. I told her that I'm not able to do anything else. I'm an outcaste. She hasn't told anybody else in the family; all my other relatives think I sell toys. I haven't told her I'm not married. I don't think she would be able to live with that, and she would not accept my children. So nobody knows that I'm not married to the man I live with. Everyone thinks he's my husband, including me.

I feel safe begging because my husband never lets me out of his sight. He watches out for me and protects me. He doesn't trust me to go alone, and is suspicious that I may meet somebody else, so he treats me well on the streets. For some women it's more difficult and unkind things sometimes happen to them.

Offered work in town
Thinks she has escaped marriage
She is trafficked

I was born 45 years ago in a Hindu Dalit community outside Maharashtra. My father worked as a forest guard for the government and my mother stayed at home to look after her six children. When I was 12 years old, I met a lady standing outside my school who told me that I had been chosen to help young children in Pune to go to school. She said: "You are literate. This is why I am taking you away, to help other children become educated." She offered to pay me Rs. 3000 a month ($75). Because there was so much poverty in my home and I was soon to be married, I decided to go. I thought it was a good way of escaping marriage. The gods had answered my prayers. So I went home, packed a small bag and left with the woman, who was waiting for me at the edge of the village. She was accompanied by a man and took me straight to a house in Bombay where there were many other young girls like me. It was a long and tiring journey but I was excited. I thought I would be able to send money home to my family and they would forgive me for running away.

I was left at the house and the couple who took me there disappeared. The house was very big and had a long hall divided into many rooms with sari cloth. I was taken upstairs and given something to eat. When I asked for the man and woman who brought me, the people just ignored me and left me alone in a room. On the second day, when I asked again for the people who brought me there a lady said: "We have paid them Rs. 18,000 ($450), so you belong to us now. If you want to leave, you must pay this money back." I was very confused and cried a lot. I didn't know what all this meant.

The next day I saw a lot of girls lined up in the nude waiting to have a shower. I began to feel strange and wondered if these were the girls I would be helping. Then someone came to my room and gave me some scanty clothes to wear. I asked: "How can I wear these clothes and do my work?" "You just wear these so that men can take you for work," a lady replied. Next they gave me creams and make up. But I said: "No, I won't wear these things." "Shut up," they said, and then they beat me up.

On the fourth or fifth day, I was sent off with a man who had paid money for me. Next time they tried to send me off with a man I said: "No! I'm not going." "If you don't go we will cut your breasts off." After this I began working as a sex worker, giving most of my money to the madam who ran the brothel. If I earned Rs. 2,000 ($50), I would get to keep only Rs. 200 for myself. Sometimes the men took me to hotels or on outings, and occasionally on holiday. But I was never allowed out with a man on my own. The madam of the brothel didn't trust any of her girls, so I was always followed by somebody. Many of the other girls who worked at the brothel had been cheated and lied to like me, but there were also many young girls from Nepal who had come voluntarily, and often their brothers or fathers would come and visit them.

When I completed my eighteenth year I became pregnant by one of my clients, and that was the first time I began to think about my parents. After my daughter turned two, I found the courage to travel back to my village. But this was the last time I saw my family. People in the village wanted to know who my child belonged to. My brothers had found out what had happened to me, and refused to accept me. My parents said: "You are dead for us, and we are dead for you."

I returned to Bombay, but decided to leave the brothel. I had paid my money back to the madam with gold and money that some of my clients had given me, and I had managed to save Rs. 35,000 ($850) secretly. I placed my child in a hostel, so she could have education and be looked after, as I had enough money to pay for this. Then I ran away from the brothel with one of my clients. He told me he loved me, and took me to Pune. But after a week of staying in a hotel, he left and went back to Africa. I didn't know what to do, so I asked a rickshaw driver to take me to the red light district. He took me to a much better brothel where I only had to pay the madam 50 per cent of my wages, and where we had proper clean rooms to work in. The madam treated her girls much better. In Bombay we were never fed properly, and never cared for if we fell ill. I earned more money in my first two years of being in Pune than I did in the eight years I was in Bombay. I worked in the sex industry till my daughter was educated to college standard and married.

I had come across a non-government organisation (NGO) that was working in the centre of Pune. Whenever my brothel got raided, or the police gave me problems, I could go and visit them at any time of the night and get help. I felt inspired by their work, and felt I wanted to help young girls in the same position I was in when I was their age. In the villages and rural areas like the one where I grew up the only opportunity for girls is marriage at 12, so many of them run away to keep their independence. They survive on the streets by begging, or are picked up on the railway stations by people who are looking for young sex workers. Many young girls come to Pune station, because trains from all over India go there. Arriving alone, carrying a small bag, looking confused, they are an obvious target for the traffickers. Within five minutes of arriving a girl can vanish and be taken away to the red light district. My daughter could have been one of these young girls if I didn't have the money to educate her.

Now that she is married, I don't have to work any more. I was always tense about the work I did, and often felt depressed. I had no self-confidence and felt I was constantly living a lie. But now I am a volunteer peer worker with the NGO that helped me, while trying to make a living from domestic work, and selling jewellery and saris on the market. I am allocated an area in the city to take care of. I give women safe sex demonstrations, showing them how to put a condom on. I make them aware of how important it is to keep their homes clean if they are working from home, and I teach them about sexually transmitted diseases and AIDS. When women have small children, I inform them about hostels they can pay for to educate and support their children. This is one of the benefits of sex work; women can afford to educate their children. If they are responsible and don't allow their children to be brought up in this difficult environment they will have the opportunity to get a professional job. If women are trying to leave the brothels, we try to help them find a husband to marry. If I ever come across a young girl working, I report it to the NGO and the police, and sometimes we try to get her married off.

Doing this work makes me feel good. I am pleased to be serving other women, and helping them to feel strong and independent. Most of the women who do this work come from poor backgrounds. You will find every caste of women working in this profession, but we are mostly from low caste Hindu families and Nepal. One of the problems we have is when women want to leave the brothels. If the madams suspect this, they lock them up, and their only way out is to make a rope out of their sari and climb out of a window. But when a woman has been seen, she is sometimes so scared that she jumps off the rope, sometimes breaking her back or limbs and sometimes not surviving.

Many of these women were once young girls who were cheated like me. Whenever I see a young girl working in the red light district I try to help her. I won't let what happened to me happen to them. It's hard to help the younger ones, though, because there is nowhere to take them. I normally work with sex workers who are between the ages of 25 and 55. It's hard doing this work as I earn much less money from this and the cleaning I do. I had many more rupees when I worked in the brothels. But if I can save even one young girl from my experience, it's worth it. I can live an honest life without looking behind my back any more. I am no longer an outcaste. I can be open with my daughter now and help her with her children.

Happy and Discontented with the Gods

Proud to be Hindu
I believe in all the gods
My life is peaceful

My parents must have told me how old I was, but I don't remember. Who in my life cares about my age? Nothing has ever been written about it, and nobody celebrates it. I know I must be nearly half-way through my fourth decade, but my age isn't very important. I am from a Hindu village near Lonavala, and I believe in worshipping the gods because they help to bring peace into my life. When I offer some of the food I cook, I can ask the gods for happiness. But I also know I have to work hard to get all the things I ask the gods and goddesses for.

I am from the *Koli* caste, and most of the people in my village are from this downtrodden caste. We are all Hindus and very proud of being so. In my village very few of the children go to school. There is no *balwadi* (kindergarten) and no big school either. Most of the children go into the jungle to pick fruit and then sell it at the market. Sometimes we offer these fruits to the gods. Many of us children used to pray to the gods in the forest, asking them to stop our parents making us work so hard. When I was ten I began working properly. My parents had five children to feed, and we all had to help with the family economy. My father packs bulbs and my mother is a servant. My brothers, sisters and I worked as child labourers on construction sites and sometimes sold wool.

As I got older my parents became frustrated with me, and made it clear they didn't want me at home any more. They wanted me to get married, so after my menses started they arranged my marriage. This was a very beautiful moment in my life. The arrangement ceremony was elaborate and beautiful. There were devotional rituals to the god Vitthal and the goddess Rukhmai. I put turmeric on my body so that I would look beautiful and young, and there was an ornament and sari ceremony where I was taken shopping for new things.

My parents are poor, so they were only able to purchase a watch for my dowry. But my in-laws were very kind. Even though the watch didn't work, they didn't pressure my family, they just sent it back to my parents without complaining. I was nervous for almost two weeks, because the tradition is that the marriage must take place within 15 days of the arrangement ceremony. It's the time when all the formalities are agreed. I prayed every day asking the gods for everything to be agreed with my in-laws.

Marriage is part of village culture. It's a big event, and all the people from the village stop work to attend. It's the time we celebrate many gods and thank them for taking care of our daughters' marriage. My mother and her sister cooked for a whole day so they could feed all the gods and goddesses and the village people.

On the day of my marriage the Brahmin came to my village and conducted the ceremony. He made a fire and called in the goddess of fire. I sat with my husband and offered sandal wood, ghee, stems of the mango plants and many more things to the fire. Then we walked around the fire seven times and took our oath in front of the Brahmin and all the village people. We promised that we would stay with each other even if we were born seven more times into this world. We promised to keep each other in our hearts and never let our minds stray. We offered saris and sacred chanting. Then the village people threw rice grains all over us. After this *puja* the Brahmin took his donation and some food in a tiffin, and left. Then all the people in the village feasted on the food which my family had prepared.

At the end of the day I left with my husband and moved into his parents' house. In the beginning it wasn't very easy because I kept thinking about my own family, and wanting to be back at home with them. It was a big change for me and I felt uneasy. I had joined a big family with two brothers-in-law and their wives, and there was a lot of work, so after a while my husband and I moved out, which made life much easier.

I have three children, a son of 7 and two daughters of 12 and 16. It's very hard to educate them all because in my husband's village there are no schools. My eldest daughter left school aged 12, because she had to walk an hour up and over a mountain to get to school. It was too much for her, so I let her do domestic work at home. The other children are still managing the walk, but the next daughter will have to stop soon, as I don't have the money to continue her studies. I'm not sure what their futures will be, but I pray to the gods and ask that they may have a better life than myself. I'm not going to hurry my children into marriage because I know it's not good for them. My eldest daughter clearly isn't ready to marry a man and live with his family. As long as she continues to help me with the work I can manage. I work in the rice fields. It's hard work at the moment as it's the season of cutting the crops down and laying them out to dry, before we gather them up into haystacks. It's also the time we remember the gods. We make sweet rice and offer it to the fields, in the hope that we will get an abundant crop and good weather. We've had strong rains and so we must remember the gods. When the rice season is over, I work in other people's kitchens. I earn Rs. 50 (60 pence) a day.

I like my employers. They are good to me. I would rather sit at home, of course, but the people I work for are Buddhist and are kind to me and my family. They treat me well and I don't feel inferior. I respect their religion and they respect mine. We are all from the same downtrodden class, we are all part of the Scheduled Caste community.

> *Offered to the gods,*
> *Khandoba, at six years old*
> *Her husband for life*

I grew up in a very poor Hindu family in the heart of Bombay. My father was unable to work because he had an illness that nobody knew how to cure, and it was very hard for my mother to feed five children. None of us went to school, and as soon as my brothers were old enough they went out to work to help to feed the family.

When I was six, I was married to the god Khandoba. This is the god that many Scheduled Caste families worship in Maharashtra. I believe Khandoba is another form of the god Shankar. I have no memory of the time of my marriage to the god because I was very young, but my mother told me about it when I completed my 12th year, because I was wondering why there was no talk of any proposals for marriage. This is what she told me. Every Sunday when I was young, all the families in my locality worshipped Khandoba, and special people used to come from his temple and knock on our doors asking for food and money. One Sunday, a man and a lady from the temple came to my house asking for gifts, and while my mother went to find something, they stepped inside our house. When my mother returned from the kitchen they pointed to my father on the bed, and asked, "What is wrong with your husband?" My mother broke down and cried, and said: "He's been sick for more than eight years. He just sleeps all day." My elder sister remembers the lady looking around the one room we lived in, pointing to me and saying: "You have three daughters. If you offer your youngest daughter to the god Khandoba for marriage, your husband will be cured."

They left after this, but on the next Sunday they returned. My mother greeted them at the door by placing one rupee on the man's forehead and 25 paise on the lady's forehead. She told the temple people: "I will offer my youngest daughter for marriage." My sister says that I was wrapped in white cloth, and turmeric was rubbed on my hands and face to prepare me for marriage. My mother had to find Rs 5,000 ($120) to give to the temple people before the marriage. She travelled to Jejuri in Pune, the famous site of Khandoba's home. He lives on top of a mountain and there are many steps which lead all the way up to his temple. My mother had to take me all the way up to the top for my ceremony. I had a proper marriage, with guests throwing many flowers and rice at me. My name was placed on a register, and the temple people told my mother that she had to remember I was married to Khandoba, and that I had to be completely loyal to this god for the rest of my life. I had a red bindi placed on my forehead and a *mangalasutra* put around my neck.

A week after my marriage my father was sitting up in bed, talking and laughing, and there was much celebration in my home. And after that, my father lived another 14 years. I knew I was a special child, but I didn't know why. I was sent away to the temple in the holidays, and I was taught to sing and dance for the gods. I learned the traditional dance of the gods, called *jagran*. I had to wear a sari and keep the scarf over my head. In the hand in which my sari scarf was held to keep it on my head I also carried a small bell. My other hand was spread out flat, and the dance involved shaking both hands in opposing ways to each other.

My older brothers didn't like it that I was dancing for the gods, and told my mother not to let me do it because it was bringing shame on the family. My mother didn't listen, so they tried to stop me attending the programmes by beating me. But I didn't care; the gods were my life, and so I continued to dance. My brothers blamed me for spoiling their life. They claimed that all their friends were teasing them and laughing at them and they insisted I must stay in the house. I would pretend to fall asleep in front of them, and once they were asleep, I would sneak out of the house so I could fulfil my duties, dancing for the gods. But sometimes in the morning they would see white powder on my face and know that I had been out. So they threw me out of my mother's house. There was nothing she could do to protect me, but she reminded me I must stay loyal to the gods. Once my brothers married I returned home, but they have refused to speak to me since I was 16. I am not considered part of their family; it's forty years since I have seen them.

After I completed my eighteenth year, I began to want to marry, as my sisters and all my friends had done. My mother said: "No, you are married to the gods." But I kept begging her to let me get married, and finally she agreed. I wasn't allowed a proper marriage; it was just a legal marriage, a marriage on paper only. There was no big arrangement ceremony, no wedding programme and no guests. I just went to the courts with my husband and signed a paper. I chose my husband myself. He was somebody I had grown up with; he knew that my loyalty was to the gods and he was happy to accept this. He died ten years or more ago, but I still have to wear my red *bindi* and *mangalasutra*. I'm not allowed to wear a black *bindi*. I must live my whole life as a married woman; I can never be a widow.

My whole life is dedicated to the gods. When I have a

problem, I close my eyes and see them, and they solve all my difficulties in life. I work for the gods performing a programme called *jagran*. We begin at 12 midday and must complete the ritual by four in the morning. We sing songs for the gods and tell their life stories. The men play *dimadi* and *tunatuna* and the ladies dance and sing. We burn seven almonds, seven coconuts, seven cashew nuts, rice and wheat in a copper pot for the gods.

Jagran is for all Hindu families. After a marriage ceremony the family must have a *jagran* programme to fulfil the wishes of the gods. This is how I earn my living today, providing *jagran*. I travel throughout Maharashtra with a group of four men and one other woman. I am in demand because I am the oldest wife of Khandoba living. Many other women have offered their daughters to Khandoba, but they do it in hope of gaining prosperity. Many of the young wives are not loyal, and do not perform their duties. I have great respect for this beautiful tradition of *jagran* and feel responsible for keeping it alive. Many people say I have made this tradition popular. I have been invited to attend many important functions to perform my duty, and the newspapers have written about my life.

I still visit my husband every full moon night at the temple, and make many offerings to him. I am happy with my service to the gods. This is what I have done my whole life. My sons support me in my work. They play the instruments and know all the traditional songs. Of course I wouldn't marry my daughters to the gods. Today things are different. My mother only did this because she needed my father to live. I am not a *devadasi*. They worship the god Yellamma, and the women who marry this god are mainly from south India. I wasn't sold into prostitution like many of these women. I am a *Murali*. In my community we are much respected.

Let down by the gods
Traditional chains – cultural ties
There's no place to run

I was born 24 years ago in a Hindu village. I am the last child of my father's second marriage. His first wife had died and that made him very short-tempered. He quarrelled with everyone in the village. He would even argue about the soil, stones and sticks outside the front door, and he was so short-tempered and rude to all the people that they stopped going to his grocery shop. We became very poor because of his temper; he had to close his shop down, and people stopped serving him in their shops. He was so troublesome that he lost our entire social and economic security. People shunned him. Although all his children were clever he had no money to educate us, so we ended up working from the age of seven.

My mother was very different. She was flexible, and trusted in the gods to support her. Because my family are Scheduled Caste, *Mahars* from Maharashtra, we couldn't worship the gods at the temples, so my mother found a living *deva* called Avdhadut whom she could follow and worship. She would pay him the little money she had for his help. Sometimes she would take me with her, and she would give him food and money and then fall down at his feet and ask him to make our life better. My mother often fasted for the gods in the hope that they would help her overcome her problems with our father.

I learned to follow this same faith, believing in all the gods, believing that it was my duty to serve the Brahmins and that I was inferior because of my karma. But I also believed that the gods could really help and change all our family's suffering. My mother told me about all the gods and goddesses, and taught me how to worship them properly. She told me that if I did this, my every wish would be fulfilled by the gods. If my wish wasn't fulfilled it would be because the gods and goddesses wished me to continue to suffer because of my karma. So I learned that the gods and goddesses had the power to create and get rid of suffering.

From the age of sixteen I began copying my mother. I would fast for the gods, and began to believe that I was full of their blessings. This was during the time that a marriage was being arranged for the last of my sisters, and I knew I would be next. I decided to worship Lakshmi, the goddess of wealth. I believed she could fulfil all my needs and wishes, and remove all my suffering. I had complete faith in her and depended on her for everything. I prayed and fasted, and asked that she give my sister a handsome and good man to marry. Even though my sister ended up with a husband who was always drunk and battered her, I still didn't lose faith. I just told myself that my sister must have very bad karma. I asked Lakshmi to take me out of my poverty, and to stop my mother and father from fighting. But none of my wishes came true, and so I became frustrated with life, although I did have some hope that something would change. I began searching for something. I didn't know what it was, but I knew there must be a better life than the one I and the other *Mahar* people in my village were living. These thoughts kept me alive.

I was married shortly after my sister, and I thought that perhaps at least one prayer had been answered, and that the gods had sent me a kind young handsome man. This strengthened my faith even more, and when we set up house, I built a big shrine to Lakshmi and wrote many letters to her, placing them at her feet. After a few months of marriage my husband began coming home drunk and beating me, so I wrote to Lakshmi asking her for a healthy, happy life and the removal of my husband's bad habits. One day my husband's brother came to visit our new home, and he seemed shocked. He said, "You are an intelligent woman. Why do you write such letters to these gods? Haven't you heard of Ambedkar and Buddhism? This is the way for our people." He refused to come into my home after that day. But he would keep ringing me and telling me about retreats happening during Diwali.

After he'd been putting pressure on us for a year, my husband and I decided to go on retreat. I was so impressed with everything. I loved the altar with the Buddha on it. I enjoyed all the chanting, singing and ritual in the *dhamma* hall, and the discipline. I had never felt like this while praying to and worshipping Lakshmi. I felt blissful. I didn't understand what the meditation was about, or any of the Buddhist texts they read. I just had this overwhelming feeling of inspiration and faith. I was pregnant on this first retreat, and I knew that it was essential for me to be careful what I listened to, because my child would be receiving it too.

Somebody gave me Dr. Ambedkar's book *The Buddha and His Dhamma*. I began to read it, and immediately knew that I was reading the truth. I learned that the Buddha was a human being and I realised that there were no gods, and that we are all equal as human beings. This was shocking to me, because I had grown up believing that I was inferior to all the Brahmins and high caste people, that I had to worship them, and that I must worship all the gods and goddesses.

This retreat also showed me that there was no difference between men and women. I couldn't believe it when I listened to women chanting the Buddha *puja*, because it was so difficult to pronounce. I had grown up to believe that all the hard work is done by men, and that women just do simple things. I felt so proud of the women reciting the *puja* by heart that I wanted to learn it too. I wanted to change, become a different woman. But I think my husband was frightened by all the new things he saw, because he began drinking on the retreat and left it halfway through.

It was all very frightening to me. I went home from the retreat feeling inspired, but also very afraid. I wanted to do in my life what I had learned on the retreat. But I was scared because in my Hindu culture it's a woman's duty to give birth, clean, cook, wash, and worship the gods. These are the only things she should do. She is not meant to make any decisions about her life, or her children's life. That is all up to her husband.

My husband didn't seem so inspired. He just believed in enjoying life, eating, drinking and thinking of himself. But it did have some effect on him because he behaved very well towards me for three months after the retreat was over. He still drank, but he didn't touch me or hit me. But he was drinking all the money we had to buy food. He couldn't afford to keep me, and sent me back to my parents for the delivery of my first child. But my parents sent me back once my daughter had been born, and my husband was in a very bad state. There was no bed or cushions for me to sleep on, and no food for any of us to eat. When I complained he began beating me with sticks, and took scissors and knife to me. He was beating me every day and not giving me or the baby any money for food. I lost my mental state for a while, and I began worshipping the gods more than I had ever done before. I believed that if I was generous to them, this would ensure the end of all my difficulties.

Some of my friends in the village saw what was happening, and took me to the hospital. I told the doctor that my husband was trying to kill me and my child. This made things worse, because people began to call me a mad woman, and I lost my mind even more. Eventually the doctor gave me an injection and sent me to my parents' house. I was unconscious and mentally disturbed most of the time I was there. When my husband beat me, I couldn't shout out because he didn't want the neighbours to know what was happening. So my screams and voices stayed in my head, and began to start shouting out aloud and begging the gods for help when I walked the streets. I didn't share my sorrow with anybody. This was why I was so blocked and broken down. I lost my mind for a while.

The doctor was supportive and did try to speak to my husband and tell him to take proper care of me, and give me no trouble. When my first child was seven months old, I managed to find the strength to return to my husband's house. I had support from some of the people I had met on the retreat, and they encouraged me to stop worshipping the gods and go to *Dhamma* classes once a week. My husband became interested in Buddhism too because his brother put pressure on him, and together we learned about the teachings of the Buddha. I was invited to become a *Dhammamitra* (a friend of the *Dhamma*) in 2004 by the TBMSG who were doing some work in my village. But this had a terrible effect on my husband, because a woman should not be seen to be higher than a man in Hindu culture. After my after this event, he took me home and hurt me with scissors and knives. These are the scars.

After this he changed. Sometimes he behaved like a human being and then he would become an animal. He had an ego problem. He wanted everything I wanted. Six months later he was invited to become a *Dhammamitra* too and for a few weeks he behaved well to me. But then once again he started beating me till I dropped to the floor. And that's still the situation. Although my *Dhamma* friends try to support me, and encourage me to try to sort the problems out, it is very hard. Sometimes I feel like running back to the gods and goddesses, but I know in my heart they can't help me because they never did before. I stay with my husband because in Indian tradition you stay with your husband forever. I still sometimes fear the gods will punish me if I leave. But I also stay because I have three children. If I leave it may affect my children's development, and my parents are too poor to be able to support me.

My husband has a very sad story. His father disappeared and his mother committed suicide when he was about seven. All his brothers and sisters were sent to different relatives. He stayed with friends of the family and they didn't give him any love or affection. He didn't learn what a proper family is. He grew up with great hatred and anger in his heart, and began drinking away his pain from the age of ten.

My faith in the Buddhist teachings keeps me strong. I have learned that both happiness and sorrow arise from within us, and that it is possible to change my suffering. The teachings of the Buddha help me to live my life. I have also learned that I can't expect my husband to look after my children and I must do this myself. Because of the TBMSG I have managed to get my children a good education in a school where I don't have to pay fees. My husband still drinks and beats me, but I try to be different. When I don't have soap or food, I teach my children not to worry, these are only material things, and material things are not what make people happy in life. Because my husband drinks so much we don't have money to have proper utensils in the house, or food, so I am ashamed to invite people round. But I realise these are my thoughts. It's not the gods punishing me because of my bad deeds. My friends wouldn't judge me this way. I realise I have to let go of material needs. That sort of thinking is still me being dependent on the gods.

I try my hardest not to waste my money on food and gifts for the gods, who have never done anything to help me in my life.

'The Rise and Fall of the Hindu Woman'

How the scriptures have oppressed Indian women

As in many ancient civilisations throughout the world, at one time the Indian woman was equal to men. She was highly respected, had access to education, and could read and learn the religious scriptures. "In ancient India (3200-2500 BC) the caste system was non-existent since even the most learned men were good householders and had varied occupations. The women of ancient India were just as good as men in learning, education and intellect. The choice of a woman's mate was according to her own wishes, and marriage was practised after the coming of age. She attended parties, competitions and religious functions as she wished. The remarriage of young widows was also a common practice."[13]

Since that time, scriptures like the *Manusmriti*, the *Bhagavad Gita* and the *Ramayana* have all sanctified an enslavement of Indian women and an erosion of their basic human rights. In his article 'The Rise and Fall of the Hindu Woman: Who Was Responsible For It?' Ambedkar writes: "Who was responsible for it? It was Manu the Law Giver of the Hindus. There can be no other answer."[14] He goes to great lengths in his article to show that the Buddha tried to ennoble Indian women, and that he wanted them to be on the same level as men. Ambedkar believed that the *Sudras* and women were the two groups who flocked to the Buddha, undermining the Brahminic religion. Manu's laws, in his view, were an attempt to prevent these groups from leaving Brahminism. Whether or not this can be proved, what is clear is that the laws in the *Manusmriti* continue to influence how women are treated today. And the woman who suffers most is the Dalit woman. The majority of these women are uneducated, slaves to the caste Hindus, and solely dependent on their husbands for their basic needs. The laws of Manu forbid all economic, political, social and educational advancement of women.

In the lowest castes educating daughters is still not valued today, despite the fact that the government has introduced reservations (reserved places in education) for all Dalit children. In 2000 the National Commission for Scheduled Castes and Scheduled Tribes reported that 25 per cent of Dalit girls dropped out of education at primary school level. Many women who live in the villages and the slums still believe that their daughters don't need an education. Why waste money on her when she'll marry, have children and go to live with her in-laws? Since the majority of Dalit families live below the poverty line, their daughters are often married by the age of 14, so that they are no longer a financial burden on the family. In the really poor segments of society, girl children are often only educated to the age of nine, and then they are under pressure to look after their younger siblings.

According to Manu, women were born to seduce men and because of this a woman must be controlled vigilantly by the males in her family. She had no right to divorce either. The *Manusmriti* states that a woman must be dependent on the males in her family day and night. It says: "In childhood a female must be subject to her father, in youth to her husband, when her lord is dead to her sons. A woman must never be independent."[15] The Dalit woman is still often dependent on her husband to the extent that she will rarely travel anywhere on her own, unless she has to go out to work. She is married off to her husband and then goes to live with her in-laws and serve her husband's family. If her sons never marry they stay at home with her, and she looks after them until she dies. And if her son does marry, he will bring his wife home.

If she is widowed, she is not allowed to marry again, and the ancient practice of *sati*, in which the wife has to climb onto her husband's funeral pyre and be burned with his body, is now illegal. This practice was meant to maintain endogamy, ensuring that the widow would not intermarry. Widowhood was a threat to the endogamous *jati* system because although nobody from her own *jati* would want to marry a widow, it is possible that a man from the same *varna* but a different *jati* might offer marriage, especially if he had been widowed or was having difficulty finding a wife. Though this custom of widow burning was declared illegal in British India 1829, there are still occasional cases of *sati* reported in India today. In October 2006 a paper reported the case of a woman in Rajasthan who was reported missing; her remains were found on the funeral pyre of her husband. The families who commit such atrocities do it because they believe they are living in accordance with the sacred scriptures. "Only last year in 2005, in Madhya Pradesh, there was a case where there was a community who were trying to force a wife to take *sati*. The police tried to intervene, and the people insisted that the police leave them alone because this was their traditional custom."[16]

Manu reduced the woman to the status of a slave, and even gave permission for men to beat their wives. Domestic violence is a big issue in Indian society. Rape within marriage is quite common. Often men force their wives to have sex; the husband feels it's his right and her duty because she is his wife. He may beat her, and she rarely says anything to anyone about it, because that would bring shame upon her. In any case, there is nowhere for her to go as she has no economic independence. Both men and women have grown up in a culture in which, as the *Manusmriti* states, "Him to whom her father may give her, or her brother with the father's permission, she shall obey as long as he lives and when he is dead, she must not insult his memory."[17]

The women I interviewed repeatedly told me that if their husbands were beating them and they had fled to their families, their parents would not listen to their complaints and would send them back home. They sometimes lived in fear of their lives, they told me. Sadly this is still the case for many women today. Some even take their own lives to escape this torture, or are burned alive because a dowry has not been paid. "In many of today's rural villages every year you will find that two or more women are murdered by dowry burning or commit suicide to escape their marriages."[18] Manu states that the killing of a woman is a minor offence, and it seems that even today parents would prefer their daughter to end up dead in her husband's home than come to her rescue and deal with the shame of a failed marriage. Women have literally told me, we are like *chappals*, which means 'sandals'. For a woman to say that her husband treats her like a *chappal* shows how insulted and demeaned she feels, as the sandal is the lowest part of the body, and dirty. Most women are treated as a man's possession; men treat women as if they can do with them what they like.

"A woman is burned, beaten to death or driven to commit suicide, officials say. Overall, a crime against women is committed every three minutes in India, according to India's National Crime Records Bureau."[19]

On October 26, 2006 a new law was passed to make the home safe for women. A man can now be charged for physically abusing, beating, pushing or shoving his wife; for sexual abuse, forcing his wife to have intercourse or looking at pornography·

for verbal abuse, if he insults her, and economic abuse, if he is not providing for his wife and children. This new act also includes dowry demands and threats, and men can be jailed for up to one year, or fined Rs. 20,000, ($480), or both, for their crimes. But the majority of victims live in the villages and slums, are illiterate and do not read newspapers or own televisions, so they will be unaware of these new rights and will remain victims of Manu's laws.

Ambedkar wanted an end to all of this. He wanted an end to the dowry system. He was against marriage between a 12-year-old girl and a 30-year-old man. He wanted women to be equal to men, and in one of the rousing speeches he delivered at the All India Depressed Classes Women's Conference to 25,000 Dalit women on July 20, 1942, he said: "Do not be in a hurry to marry. Marriage is a liability. You should not impose it upon your children unless they are financially able to meet the liabilities arising from marriage. Those who will marry should bear in mind that to have too many children is a crime. The parental duty lies in giving each child a better start than its parents had. Above all, let each girl who marries stand up to her husband, claim to be his friend and equal and refuse to be his slave."[20]

Child marriage is still common in the villages and the slums. Given that over half of India's population still live in slums and villages, the issue of child marriage is thus still a huge concern. On September 25, 2006 a state newspaper reported that in Pune, the second largest city in the state of Maharashtra, on average 500-600 child marriages take place every year. Most of these girls will have grown up in the slums inhabited by the Dalit communities. However, the situation is changing in some parts of the community. "Since conversion, child marriage in the Buddhist community has dropped. Compared to some communities, many Buddhists are marrying their daughters at an older age."[21]

Things have changed in India in the last ten years. There is a fast-growing and wealthy middle class. India has been very much more under the influence of Western culture and multinational industries, and access to world media through internet, satellite and other technology has had a huge cultural impact, especially on the high caste educated Hindu woman. Western women's magazines have flooded the market, and Indian women are being exposed to headlines like 'Ten ways to have a good orgasm', in a culture that is extremely modest about the naked body. High class and upper middle class women can now be seen in hotels drinking beer and smoking cigarettes, which would have been almost unthinkable ten years ago. These women have become independent through education, are making choices about how many children they will have, pursuing professional careers, and adopting Western cultural social behaviour.

But Indian society still continues to be mainly patriarchal, and it is the women in the lower castes who are most affected. These women are socialised to feel inferior. The birth of a son is the cause of a celebration, but the birth of a girl is still seen as a calamity, a cause of regret and disappointment. Poor families keep having children until they produce a son. There is much female foeticide, and in places like Rajasthan, when daughters are born they are sometimes burned alive. Even if she is allowed to live, fathers often don't acknowledge the birth of a female child. It's the sperm which determines whether a baby is a boy or a girl, but even though this is a biological fact, it's the woman who gets blamed if she does not produce a male heir. Some husbands take a second wife in the hope that she will give him a son.

In some parts of India, Dalit girls are sold into the Hindu *devadasi* system to alleviate the family's poverty. They are married to Hindu gods on full moon night, and become servants of the gods. Such a girl becomes the property of the temple, serving the Brahmin priest, who has first right to sleep with her, to save himself from being polluted. She is sexually exploited and ends up becoming a sex worker, and when she matures into her 20s she is often sold to the brothels.

It is hard for the Indian woman to escape this gender oppression. In some states of India, once a woman is married, she wears a red *bindi* on her forehead, a *mangalasutra* (gold and black beads) around her neck, and a silver ring on her toe, indicating she is married. The husband wears nothing like this to show his marital status, but even an educated woman will wear at least one of these things, because it is a great taboo not to. Her husband will insist she conform to this Hindu tradition, whether she was born Hindu, Muslim, Christian or Buddhist. If she is widowed, she must remove all these things, and wear a black *bindi* on her forehead, to indicate that nobody must look at her.

The main reason why most Dalit women are unable to emancipate themselves like some of their high caste sisters is because most of them still live in the villages or have migrated to the cities for work and have ended up in the slums. A woman is either a slave in her own home or, if she goes out to work, can find only the most menial type of work. Her occupations in the cities are washing pots, cooking and cleaning for others, sewing saris, weaving, leather working, digging up the roads and labouring. In the villages she works as an agricultural labourer, fisherwoman, scavenger, or disposer of human waste. Unless they have a high standard of education, it is almost impossible for Dalits, girls or boys, to get a respectable job. Educated Dalits are part of a minority who have created a tiny middle class among themselves, but they still face discrimination in the workplace. However, education is proving to be crucial in helping to change the life of the Dalit woman, because if she continues through to degree level she has the opportunity of being financially independent, and also becomes more aware of her basic human rights and that there is a way out of the slum and village mentality. Education was one of Ambedkar's great contributions, through the establishment of reserved places for Dalits in all public academic institutions. Today, though, these reserved places are under threat because of a trend towards the privatisation of education.

Buddhism has also begun to change the situation of Dalit women. Although only a minority of Dalits have converted, among this community there is a small population who have been able to throw off their Hindu conditioning and accept that it's a person's worth which is important, not their birth. They no longer feel oppressed by the interpretation of the law of karma which states that they can do nothing about their situation in life. They have been told that they are born to serve because of bad deeds they have committed in their past lives, but they have proved the theory wrong and have empowered themselves to achieve great things, like Ambedkar himself.

While there is indication of Dalit women empowering themselves, the problem is that the majority of them still live in the villages and the slums, and in these environments the oppression of females is strong. Most of the villages will be unaware of new laws to support women, and most girls will be married off by the time they are 16.

Ambedkar chose Buddhism because it challenges this negative theory of karma and gives all people, men and women, access to the scriptures and spiritual development. He and those who joined his movement set up educational hostels for Dalit children so they could be properly educated and uplift themselves from the status they had been born into. He realised that education could throw off the shackles of slavery.

Trailokya Bauddha Mahasangha Sahayak Gana or TBMSG is one Buddhist organisation which has continued Ambedkar's legacy by setting up hostels for children who live in villages and rural parts of India where they have no access to education. These hostels give them the opportunity to study, and provide their food and meet their other basic needs so they can attend schools nearby. However, despite being Buddhist, having been founded by Westerners, and having Buddhist ethics, TBMSG is still hampered by the patriarchal system that exists in India. There are far more hostels for boys than for girls. Social conditioning is such that women in TBMSG are still experiencing the oppression of Indian culture. Men have most of the management positions and make all the important decisions of this spiritual movement. "TBMSG has forgotten Ambedkar's philosophy on women. In Mumbai, in the area where I was born, all the men have the jobs of responsibility, they are all management. There is no proper work for women. Nobody cares about my ideas. They say: 'You're a woman. Just listen.' The men give talks about Babasaheb saying that women are very important and that they must have the opportunity to learn, but they don't give us that opportunity. They give interesting talks about women and equality but they want every job and every position for themselves. In the whole of India men behave like this, both in the house and outside. We are still victims of Hindu conditioning."[22]

There are women involved in TBMSG who are trying to help other women to realise their qualities and discover what they have to give to society and their community, trying to show them that even if they are housewives and have no education, they can still be successful in their lives. "We have to start from where most of us are, in the slums and the villages. We have set up single-sex trusts to help Dalit women who come from these social backgrounds. We are teaching them to save money, teaching them how to become independent by setting up sewing businesses, and offering education to some of their children. We can see that on the outside some women have changed, wearing good saris and expensive jewellery, but mentally these women are still weak. We have to teach them that education is far more important than good clothes and jewellery."[23] TBMSG is part of a whole social movement of non-government organisations which are trying to improve the conditions of India's approximately 250 million Dalits, who need education, slum rehabilitation, and improved living conditions in villages, medical facilities and health education.

There are many examples of heroic Indian women who have been brave enough to stand up and fight for their people. Savitri Phule from the OBC, the wife of the social revolutionist Jyotirao Phule in the 19th century, was the first Indian woman to be educated. Her husband educated her and then encouraged her to educate other women. Women felt so threatened by her that they threw cow dung in her face and tried to sabotage her work. But with determination she continued and paved the way for all Indian women to be educated. She led the way for OBC and Dalit women, so that by the time Ambedkar was campaigning there were women who were confident enough to play a major part in his movement.

In 1920 Venbai Barkar and Renubai Shambharakar were among the eloquent speakers who came to centre stage and organised women. Jaibai Chaudhari became a teacher and started Chokhamela Kanyashala at Nagpur in 1924. In 1927, Shantabai Shinde was prominent in the burning of the Manusmriti. In this same year, Geetabai Gaitwad became superintendent of the Ramabai Ambedkar boarding school, and later became a member of the Nasik municipality. In 1929 Jamubai Kamble led one of the groups in the Parvathi Mandir Satyagrabha, where 27 women were arrested. In the following year there were around 500 women who took part in the Kalaram temple movement. Ramabai, Ambedkar's wife, Seetabai and Geetabai Gaitwad took care of the food.

In 1931 hundreds of women protested against castesim in Maharashtra and Radhabai Vadale told the press: "It's better to die a hundred times than to live a life full of humiliation. We will sacrifice our lives but we will win our rights." Two years later, Anjanibai Deshbhratar set up a boarding school for orphaned 'Untouchable' girl students. In 1942, 25,000 women participated in the All India Women's Conference held at Nagpur, with Indira Patil as the general secretary, Kirti Patil as chairperson and Sulochana Dongre as president. Kaushalya Baisantri was the general secretary of the Students' Organisation of the All India Scheduled Caste Federation, which Ambedkar established in 1942, and through her work its constitution was amended and published in 1955.

These are just a few of the women who have played a major part in changing casteism in India. The women in the following pages are continuing the legacy. They are some of India's heroines who have gone unnoticed.

Feminism Activism

Beaten and raped
By Hindu and Dalit men
How to change her life?

Dalit women are the most oppressed people in society
because they suffer from both male domination and
caste prejudice. How many Dalit men are aware
that our women need to be educated, and to be economically
independent? Of course all women suffer in Indian society,
but it is the Dalit woman who is at the bottom of the pile.
The life of the Dalit woman who has converted to Buddhism
is no better. Many Dalit women of my generation were born
into Buddhism. Their grandparents, like mine, converted
to Buddhism only because Babasaheb said that if we did so,
we would not die as Hindus. For that generation this was
revolutionary because they had grown up thinking the only
way they could end their 'Untouchability' was through death.
But after Babasaheb died there was nobody to teach the people
how to live a Buddhist life. They all converted, but we still
worshipped Hindu gods and followed Hindu culture. This
is the situation of my own family. We are Buddhists but my
parents still call upon the Hindu gods and goddesses to help us,
and still celebrate all the Hindu festivals. It's the same for many
families in Maharashtra.

These festivals are mainly for women, because they are
at home doing nothing else. There is no other entertainment
for them. Their whole identity is bound up in the Hindu
festivals. Every month there is a festival, and it's the women

who engage with them, prepare the food and worship the gods and goddesses. This is how the average woman spends her life. They follow blind faith and know nothing else. Every day they go to the temple and perform rituals. All this oppresses the Dalit woman, because it keeps her waiting for the gods and goddesses to change her situation of poverty, domestic violence and inferiority.

Dalit women suffer throughout their whole life; their development is squashed. They are on the ground level, and have no chance to empower themselves. In rural India the Dalit woman has to do much hard work. She works at home, she works outside on the farm, and she looks after the children. And the men, what do they do? She also has the burden of being raped by high caste Hindu men when she is working in the fields. In such bad conditions, how can Dalit women survive? They are human beings, not animals. But if they work as farm labourers, when the upper caste women see them, they don't think: "She's a woman like me." They treat them really badly, and sometimes encourage their husbands and sons to abuse them.

How will this situation change? I have observed from working with women's groups, and researching my doctorate looking at the issues of Dalit women in India, that their condition is like this because of the women themselves. They don't speak up and say: "I will not accept these injustices." They think: "I'm a woman. I have to follow the gods. I'm a woman. It's my responsibility to take care of the house. I'm a woman. It's my responsibility to take care of the children." This is their mentality. And till this mentality changes, women are not going to change their subordinate position in society. They are helpless and have no self-esteem.

When a son is born, sweets are distributed in the house and among the neighbours and there is great rejoicing. But when a girl is born people cry, because they will have to give money for her dowry, and take care of her because she is a female. This gender bias begins right from the womb. If any Indian woman has enough money to have a scan to see what gender her unborn child is, some will have an abortion if it's a girl. There is nowhere that we females are safe. A girl is at risk in the womb and she is at risk when she is born. While growing up she is under her father's control, when she gets married she is ruled by her husband and her in-laws, and in her old age she is dominated by her sons. When her son marries he will bring his wife home to live with her, and if he never marries he will never leave his mother's house and he will be looked after by her. So everywhere men assert their power. A woman's whole life is dominated by male society.

She has no opportunity to think for herself. Women are like donkeys blindly following this life. Older women teach girls: "You are a girl, you sit like this. You wear clothes like this. You can't be manly. You have to look pretty. You can't be brave, only men can be brave. You have to be dependent on men the entire time." So women always have this feeling of inferiority. They're not confident, they think they can't do anything, and they think they have to be dependent on men their whole life.

Educated women like me must get together. We should have a group, prepare our own agenda and discuss how we want society to be. Everything should be equal for men and women. Both girls and boys should have good food and education. Girls should have the same facilities. When I look at my own children, I have to be aware of this. I have a girl and boy, and I am bringing them up in the same way.

Even though my husband is prepared to change he is a male person who grew up in Indian society with all the conditioning that brings. He still believes that men are superior so I often struggle with him. I have to tell him: "Don't give me the subordinate position." I have challenged my husband and told him: "I'm not wearing a sari every day, they are not practical. I'm not wearing a scarf over my head, and after ten years of marriage, I can wear what I like." Someone has to be bold and dare to challenge their husband, and it must be those of us who have the power of education. I tell him he can't treat our daughter differently. All the time I'm challenging him. Other women like me need to do this in their families. If we give these thoughts of equality to our children, we will create a new generation of men and women. Hopefully my son will not treat his wife in the way my husband has tried to treat me. Hopefully he won't think of inequality, because he has been taught that his sister is equal to him. Hopefully the future generations of women will not suffer. It is possible to change the male domination of society.

Seven years ago I was working with mainly Dalit women who were HIV Positive. Their living condition was so bad that healthcare was very difficult. So many women are thrown out of their houses. Their husbands blame them for their positive status. They are beaten by their husbands and beaten by their in-laws. Our women get married very young, which means that they are becoming HIV Positive in their teens. When this happens to a woman, it is the end of her life. She has no money for medicine. She is thrown out of the home. She has to go to her parents' place, but if there is a brother still at home he may complain, so sometimes she is homeless. Many people are dying because of AIDS, and the children are orphaned. We have to open up more orphanages.

I found out that the majority of people who were being diagnosed with AIDS were from the Dalit community. It made me hurt inside, and I thought, why are all my people Positive? Why do so many of them have AIDS? The reason is that the

Dalits live in the slums of the city, and have no education around sex and sexuality. The whole day the men work, and then they buy alcohol at the end of the day. They want enjoyment, and don't want to be under the burden of the family, so they go out and pay for sex from prostitutes. The husbands who are lorry drivers pass this virus up and down the country because they have sex with women in every town they stop and sleep in.

Many women in the slums are already suffering from domestic violence, and when they get Positive status the violence increases. The mother-in-law will claim that her son is very good, and it's because his wife sleeps with other men that this virus has affected him. Often a woman is beaten so badly that her bones are broken and she is hospitalised. If you ask her what happened, she will say: 'I fell down the stairs.' She will never say: 'My husband has beaten me' because she's afraid that if she complains about her husband she will be thrown out of her house. Then where will she go? If this happens, the woman has no status in society. If she's at her parents' place, people will ask: 'Why is your daughter at home?' When a daughter leaves her husband's home to go back to live with her parents, this means she is bad, her husband has thrown her out. People don't see what her husband is doing. Nobody will say it's because her husband is beating her that she is at her parents' house.

A new domestic violence act was passed this year on 25th October 2006. This is critical because everywhere this violence is happening, although usually women won't talk about it. Their mindset is that they think it's natural and OK to be beaten. But it's not natural. We are human beings, not slaves; why should we be beaten up? In many homes I have seen women suffering from domestic violence. They are also insulted by their husbands, they are deprived of food, and their husbands force them to have sex. These women suffer mental, sexual, physical, and economic harassment in their homes. And these are the four grounds that the new domestic violence act has introduced. Women can go and say: 'My husband is not taking care of us, not giving me money,' and he can be prosecuted. She can say her husband has raped her in marriage and he will no longer be in the right. Often when the woman doesn't want to have sex with her husband, he forces her because it's his wish. Under the past law she wasn't able to say no. She couldn't say it was rape because he was her husband and he had every right to do with her what he wished. But now women can go to the police.

Of course it is educated women who will benefit most from this act, but it's our duty to convey this information to illiterate women, to go to the grass roots level and tell these women about their rights. The women in the villages don't read the papers; they don't know what acts parliament has passed. My concern is how the act will be implemented, because if a woman goes to the police and complains, she will not be safe in her family. The Dalit woman always lives with her in-laws and her husband's community.

So there is still much more to be done for the rights of women. It's a process, and things will change slowly. Women are psychologically depressed because of the oppression of the family and society. We are in need of counselling centres which are near the slums the women live in. The trouble is that there's a culture that you keep all your problems in your home. You don't even take them to your parents, because they will say: "Go home, these are your problems, don't bring them here. You leave your husband's home only when you're dead."

There is much work to be done, and it must come from the Dalit woman who has had the privilege of education. We need to begin in our own homes. My message to all Dalit women is: "Change your mindset." Women like me must tell oppressed women what their rights are and how they can get out of their terrible conditions. No god is going to help them. It is only by helping themselves that their conditions will change.

> *I'm fighting for the*
> *Rights of all Dalit women*
> *Until my last breath*

I am 63 years old and I still continue to work for my people. I am president of the women's wing in the Republican Party, which fights for Dalit rights in the whole of Maharashtra. I am also secretary of a women's union which helps with the rights of women hawkers who sell on the streets of Mumbai, and I work for an insurance company trying to educate women to begin insuring for their futures.

I was born into the Scheduled Caste – I was a so-called Hindu *Mahar* – but my parents were educated and ardent followers of Dr. Ambedkar. They told me that he was the only person who had given our people freedom from the four *varnas*. They said that when a high caste Hindu is trying to push me away from them, I should remember that I also have two hands and two eyes.

In their lives they experienced slavery of the worst kind. There have been improvements, but we're still discriminated against. Many Hindus are just superficial with us. They are still living by the rules of the *Manusmriti*. The people who live by this Hindu rule book are still harassing people. Just before Ambedkar's 50th anniversary, a Buddhist family was killed by high caste people because they were not prepared to accept their religion. They want us Dalits to be suppressed; they don't want us to move above our so-called station. They want us to die in the low caste we were born in. This is their blind belief. In their minds we are still 'Untouchable', whether we have converted to Buddhism or not.

In the villages the high caste people still live in the centre, and there are still boundaries between the high caste and the low caste people. The Dalit people cannot enter their area or walk by their well. But they let us work in their fields! You have to remember that a large percentage of Indian people still live in the villages, and Maharashtra is no different. We are still facing many 'Untouchability' problems in our state. I am fighting against so many districts in this state and other states of India too. There can only be an end to this when all our people are educated and when they have enough money to improve their living standards.

The Dalit woman also has to rid herself of blind faith. But to do that, they need to escape the influence of the *sadhus*, the priests, who tell our women: "If you worship this god, he will give you a better life, he will take you out of your poverty. If you offer a goat or a cockerel, the gods will be happy and your situation will improve." So the Dalit woman just sits there waiting for the gods to change her life; she makes no effort to change it herself.

It's our women who suffer the worst kind of slavery. The Dalit woman is the most vulnerable to rape. Because she is from the lowest caste in India, she is taken advantage of. If she tries to fight her battles or escape her marriage, she will be killed. If she tries to gain independence she will be locked up in her home. If she only bears girl children she will be blamed. Although states like Maharashtra have passed laws against this, women are still getting rid of their foetuses after they have had a scan and found out that it's a girl.

In Indian society men have all the power. In every caste, in every religion of India, women are the most oppressed. Even when we have become educated, we are still harassed and crushed. We do all the work in the house and give all our wages to the men. We are often beaten and at the mercy of our in-laws. Many a Dalit woman still lives in the village where the old Hindu tradition of caste is a part of her life. If she escapes to the slums, her life is still hell – just a different hell. There she lives in humane conditions, not even fit for a pig. Her husband is most probably an alcoholic, and she has to send her children out to work by the age of ten so they can help with providing for the family. The dowry system is a major part of her life. If her family are not able to provide her husband's family with gifts of gold, bangles, motor cycles, computers, hi-fis and televisions, her life will be at risk. She may even commit suicide, or be burned by her in-laws. This is still the situation with many women from the lowest caste of India.

All this is why I work for the lowest class, rather than taking a big professional job because of my qualifications, which have given me some freedom. I have to help educate these women, so they can at least have some freedom to try and do something with their lives. This is why I began working with women from the lowest caste of society. Most of them are not educated; they are housewives, still washing pots for other people, doing the lowest kind of work possible and vulnerable to all sorts of harassment.

My first task was to encourage women to get some education. I began by teaching them to sign their names. Many of the women I've been working with face financial problems because their husbands have run off with someone else and they have no income to raise their children. So I also established a credit society, to try and teach women to save just one rupee a day from their earnings so that they can use the money in the future. I try to help women see that if they do something today, they'll be happier tomorrow. Everybody wants money but nobody keeps it aside. I try to help them see how saving one rupee a day will help them in the future.

I'm president of the women's wing of the Republican Party. I try to put pressure on the government about dowry cases, the harassment of women, and their poverty. I am fighting the state government at present because they want to make Mumbai into the new Shanghai. They want to get rid of the slum areas and build fancy skyscrapers. Over half of Mumbai's population live in slums, and would not be able to afford the new property prices and taxes. And it will be the women and their children who will be thrown out of the city.

As president, I try to make sure that women have proper reservations in elections, so that we are represented. If a woman is harassed for living in a dwelling on the street or for working as a hawker, members of my party go as a group of women and offer support. I fight cases against the police for women. Only yesterday I had a case of a woman whose husband had left her for another woman. He left her in the hut with their three children. Two days later, her brother-in-law came and snatched her hut. She is now on the streets. Even though she is married to her husband, society still seems to think that the hut she shared with her family only belongs to the husband. I have sent a letter to the police demanding they take action and give her the right to live in her hut.

There are women who have learned to make an art out of singing, but the state government has now passed an order stipulating that they can't go into bars. Police are raiding the bars because they know that one of the jobs that the uneducated Dalit woman can do to earn a decent living is singing in bars. We have tried to get this overturned, arguing that these women are not prostitutes, they are not performing naked. And what other job will society give to the Dalit woman?

There is much more that we are doing for women, and we believe that if all the Dalit parties came together as one, we

would be a stronger force in fighting our battles. I will fight for
the rights of women until my last breath.

I'm liberated
Backward birth and forward life
I have freed my mind

I was born into a Backward Class in Tamil Nadu, where there's
still a lot of discrimation against Dalits. My mother was the first
in her generation to be educated. She worked as a headmistress;
she managed to get this job because of the reserved places that
Dr. Ambedkar got for our people. My father was the manager
of a textile mill, but he died in 1991 when I was 15.

I am the youngest of seven children. All my three brothers
and three sisters are married and settled with professional
careers. I am the exception – I am the only one working in
the social work field. My mother encouraged me, and put no
pressure on me to get a government job. Through my education
and the philosophy of Dr. Ambedkar I have managed to free
my mind of the tendencies and thinking that keep my people
oppressed. I am not inferior; I was not born to stay at home,
and serve all the men in my family until I die.

At primary school, I was never segregated for being a
member of the Backward Class. I mostly related to other Dalit
children. However, before attending college, I did experience
some of the evils of casteism. The teachers would come into the
class and say, raise your hand if you are from a Backward Class
or a Scheduled Caste. If we didn't raise our hands, we weren't
allowed to have the certificate which allowed us to apply for
a scholarship so that we could continue our education. The
caste Hindu children just roared with laughter. The certificate
caused problems for many of my friends. Some refused to
put their hands up, and that was the end of their education,

they could not apply for a scholarship. Those of us who raised our hands were issued a certificate with Backward Class or Dalit stamped on it. This certificate is still issued today and it is supposed to give us our social rights. But the government authorities still use delaying tactics, and ask many questions to prove our legitimacy. Sometimes they refuse to approve the certificate because they refuse to believe that some Dalits are from the Backward Class. We were discriminated against on account of our colour as well. At school I was aware of the light-skinned students sitting together, the brown-skinned students sitting together and the black students on their own, too. It was difficult to talk to the fair students because we felt uncomfortable. From an early age I had learned to think that fair-skinned people must be superior to me. Where I grew up, if you were dark, you were a Dalit and if you were fair, you were a Brahmin.

I was an average student at college, but I wanted to prove to myself that I could do well. I became interested in Ambedkar's social movement and got involved with a literacy movement which helped to improve educational opportunities for the young Dalit children in villages and slums. When I visited the villages, I began to realise that there was a huge difference between life in the city and village life. People in the cities had many more opportunities to better themselves, and the prejudice against Dalits was not so pronounced. The poor people in the villages really needed some guidance and help. I was exposed to this discrepancy at the age of 17, so I decided not to opt for a government job, and a big fat wage and a nice house, but instead to work for the development of my people.

After this I joined a women's group and became inspired about women's issues. We talked about domestic violence and discussed dowry deaths. How is it that so many women are suddenly found dead within a few months of being married? We were concerned that so many newly-wed wives were committing suicide because they couldn't cope with the pressure. I began to look at the Hindu system I had been born into. It insists that the wife's family must give money to the husband's family. They must pay cash, give jewels, and pay for the whole wedding ceremony, which can often mean feeding hundreds of people for three or more days.

I also became a volunteer of a group called Animation, Development Employment and Communication or ADECOM. This organisation gives training to women and young people who are at the lowest level of society. Our mission is to work for the Dalit people. ADECOM opened my eyes. I knew about the practices towards my community, and had heard about caste atrocities, but I had been sheltered from the treatment of the so-called 'Untouchables' and the casteism that manifested in the villages. I soon learned that caste atrocities were not just about the Dalit community as a whole but in particular about the ill treatment of and violence against Dalit women.

I visited many villages all over Tamil Nadu while I was with ADECOM and witnessed clearly what was happening to Dalit women. They were treated much worse than Dalit men. I also saw the curse of domestic violence, how women have to live with such brutality and accept physical and sexual violence in their homes. I saw that they had nowhere to flee to. I saw how women were exploited by the high caste people. The Dalit woman was and still is the lowest paid person in the village. There is no protection for her. She has to work for the high caste Hindus in their homes and in the fields, and many of the young girls are subject to abuse. The landlords feel it's their right to enjoy the young women. They know they can get away with it because firstly, their workers are dependent on their money to feed their children and secondly, the police, who are nearly always Brahmins and other high caste Hindus, would never believe them.

This situation sickened me, and I became even more motivated to change women's lives. I began to oppose patriarchy and became very interested in feminism, to the extent that I would not accept any man in my life. But I came to realise after a few years that instead of opposing men directly, I had to oppose the patriarchal system. I decided to be open again to men, and one of my colleagues who was sympathetic to feminism pursued me. He motivated me a lot, he taught me to explore Buddhism along with Ambedkarism and feminism, and showed me how Buddhism and Ambedkarism were about the equality of all men and women. I opened up to him, and we had an inter-caste marriage. We are both Dalit, but he is from the *Sudra* caste, which is higher than the caste I was born into.

Even though I'm married I still see how important it is to continue to accept the feminist point of view and how we women have to take our own political stand. With other women I began to empower women, at a village level. Realising that grass roots democracy begins in the village, we tried to help them become involved with village politics. We help Dalit women have the confidence to stand for the village council, which is called the Panchayat. We want them to begin taking leadership roles in their lives. If women are able to sit equally with men at these meetings and raise their own basic needs, their situation could change. During the past ten years we have trained Dalit women to take power, and many of them are sitting side by side with Dalit men and Brahmins. They have learned to speak out and talk boldly about their needs at these gatherings. Before, Dalit women were not allowed to attend these meetings that made all the decisions about village life.

Now in the Pondicherry and Tamil Nadu area we have around 7,000 women leaders elected to sit in the Panchayat. We've helped them to create a democracy. This is a small beginning; there are many Dalit women who could never step into this environment owing to the entrenched caste politics of their community. And Dalit women still do not have the space to discuceess their issues at a national or state level. I believe that Dalit women have to begin stepping forward if we are to be part of the political system.

In 2006 I came together with several women to form a political group called the Women's Front. It focuses on women's participation in politics and on land issues. We believe that through our participation we will gain power for Dalit women. The Women's Front is open to all women, but only 3 per cent of our members are from the Brahmin caste. We have decided to differentiate ourselves from other female political parties by wearing pants and shirts. We believe we are also different because we are women from different castes coming together to talk about our issues at a wider level.

We realise that women must be elected at a constitutional level and we will be sending 30 women to stand for 30 districts in the Tamil Nadu locality. If they are elected, we can then run to be elected at a state level too. It is important for women to be represented at all levels of society. We aim to bring women into politics. We believe that 50 per cent of parliamentary seats should be occupied by women. If we are properly represented, our members will be able to talk about poverty, domestic violence and sexual harassment at a constitutional level, and this will give the legal mechanism to prevent atrocities like this. At present, women occupy less than 3 per cent of parliamentary seats.

Although the government says it is against the law to practise 'Untouchability', it continues in many places throughout India, because the idea of caste still prevails in the minds of many Hindus. Inter-caste marriages are still not accepted in many traditional and rural areas. Caste-based organisations and associations still exist in India and play a crucial role in perpetuating the idea of caste and the politics of caste. Caste Hindus want to see an end to government reservations policy. Caste conflicts often lead to violence, bloodshed and death. In many educational institutions and work environments, people still tend to group themselves on the basis of their caste, and Indian temples are still under the siege of caste chauvinism. Temples, many of which are managed by government officials, do not recruit men from Backward Castes to act as temple priests. Many politicians shamelessly or clandestinely seek votes in the name of caste during the general elections.

So you see, India is not free of casteism, prejudice and discrimination. The Women's Front has a lot of work to do. Ambedkar's work must be realised throughout India if we are to reclaim our dignity and human rights. Through the values and principles of Buddhism and Ambedkarism it is possible to break the patriarchal system that has oppressed Dalit women. These values will also have an effect on men, encouraging them to treat women more kindly. We need to work at an educational, political, work, social and spiritual level to gain our emancipation.

When I look at the *Mahar* caste, I can see that many of them have improved their lives, many of them are confident, and many have raised their status through becoming Buddhists. I believe that all Dalits must begin to talk about the survival of Buddhism. We must begin to accept Ambedkar's version of Buddhism. This will emancipate us and give us the autonomous life we deserve in the 21st century. Four years ago, therefore, I accepted conversion to Buddhism. We have no Buddhist groups to help teach my community, but through studying the philosophy of Ambedkar there are people in my community who have the knowledge to teach the people about Buddhism. There is great fear about Buddhism in the part of India I live in. People are afraid that if they become Buddhist, they may be ostracised, but through proper education the Dalit community will come to understand that it's about freedom from the past, about returning to something which was part of our culture thousands of years ago.

The jubilee year of Ambedkar's death inspired me to encourage people to learn more about him. I had the privilege to take part in this historic event, reciting the vows and precepts with my people from Tamil Nadu and Pondicherry on October 2, 2006 in Nagpur at the Nagaloka Institute for Buddhist training, education and meditation. Fifty-six men and thirty-six women converted to Buddhism and vowed to follow the *Dhamma* in their lives. This was a huge turning point. This conversion is important because we are talking about liberty, equality and fraternity for all people. For this reason they all accepted Buddhism for their own liberation from Hinduism. This is the largest group of people who have converted *en masse* from my community, and I am hoping that these people will become leaders, to help the thousands of Dalits back home to understand Ambedkar and Buddhism, and give them courage to convert.

October 14, 2006 witnessed the conversion of many other Dalit castes. Hundreds of thousands of people converted on that day, and this is the next major step to freeing ourselves from the atrocities of Hinduism. But much work is left for us to do. I believe it is time now for women and the Dalits of India to rise and emancipate ourselves. But we need solidarity and we must first develop action in the villages and let it evolve from there.

Dr. Ambedkar's vision of Buddhism has taught me that I must do social work for my people and not just be concerned about my own personal development. I have therefore committed my whole life to challenging prejudice and mobilising resources to develop Dalit areas. Dalit communities need to mobilise their funds and care for the whole community. This has begun in the Tamil Nadu and Pondicherry areas. We have managed to raise money to support 20 districts, in education and social development.

It is the responsibility of the educated Dalit to highlight the struggle of education, liberty, equality and fraternity. The way to achieve this is by integrating the religious with the political. Ambedkar said that our fight needs to be non-violent; we must fight for our rights in a non-violent way. As Buddhists, we can fight for our rights in a compassionate way which creates harmony and friendliness. But for many Hindus, being Buddhist means being low caste. As far as they are concerned, a Dalit is a Dalit. He or she can do nothing to change his or her caste in this lifetime. This is the struggle we face in today's India.

'Till Death Do Us Part?'

My feelings of love
My crime, shame, persecution
Blind faith – blind values

Love marriages are still not accepted among the Dalit community, and marriages between castes are even harder to accept. I am from the Buddhist community, and although casteism is not meant to exist in Buddhism, unfortunately it does. When I was 18 I fell in love with a man from the *Pan* caste; I am from another caste. We were the two Dalit castes in my village that had converted to Buddhism, and although we did business with each other, we most definitely did not share our daughters.

I met the love of my life when I was travelling on a bus to visit my brother. A man sat beside me and began speaking to me. He followed me off the bus and asked me where I was going. By coincidence he was going to the same place as me, the same house. I couldn't believe it. He seemed to know my family and accompanied me to my brother's house. I was helping to take care of things there while my brother's wife was seriously ill in hospital. This man began visiting me there, and my brother seemed to accept it. I began to feel attracted to the man, and he was definitely attracted to me. He told his friends about me, and slowly the gossip spread that he wanted to marry me. My brother heard the gossip, and he blamed me for the attraction. I didn't know what to do because I felt I hadn't done anything wrong.

One day while I was cleaning and cooking in my brother's

house, my brother and father came into the house and closed all the doors and windows so nobody could see. And then they both beat me up, blaming me for encouraging this man into my life. My father made it clear to me that he was angry because the man was from a different caste. The next day he pushed me out of the house, and sent me to my uncle's house – and my uncle hit me too. I was very disturbed because my father is an educated man, and I had listened to him give many talks at Ambedkar programmes. He always told the people that we have to end casteism and that casteism does not exist in Buddhism. And now my father was going against everything he had preached in front of thousands of people. I was also disturbed because when I was a child I had often watched my father beat my mother, and now he was doing exactly the same to me.

Since my father put so much pressure on me, I couldn't express myself. I couldn't say, I love this man and I want to marry him, because I knew that my father wanted to be in control of arranging my marriage. I felt confused because the man had proposed to me, and he expected me to say yes, but I couldn't because I knew that my father would not give me permission, and this would also put me at risk.

My father made it difficult for me to stay in the village where I grew up. He spread awful rumours about me, and I felt too embarrassed to walk out of my front door. I was full of shame. When I was sent to my uncle things were even worse. I thought life would be better in a big city like Mumbai, but my relatives made my life hell. They put me under a 24-hour house arrest for three years. I had no permission to go out alone and was never allowed to visit any of my relatives. I wasn't even allowed to see my sick brother, who died during this time. I had no way of contacting the man I loved either.

My father's brother got tired of me, so I was sent off to my mother's brother, and this uncle was very kind to me. He gave me some emotional support and was my only ally. I was able to tell him about my confusion, and he explained Dr. Ambedkar's doctrines to me thoroughly. I learned that it was Ambedkar's wish that we marry inter-caste, and that the Buddha made it clear that we were all equal, that there was no casteism in his Buddhist *sangha*. This gave me some hope.

My father began to inquire about me. He wrote letters to my uncle, and I found out that he had decided to marry me to somebody and wanted to arrange a meeting. This was extremely hard for me as I still loved the man I'd met all that time ago, but my brother had just died, so there was great pressure on me. My uncle told me I should try to be considerate and think of my mother as she had just lost a son, and would be worrying about me because I was 20 and still single. But I refused to give in. Instead I took control of my life and stopped eating so that when the men came to look at me, I looked really sick and weak. This strategy worked, as none of the men wanted me.

My father became even angrier because all the men were rejecting me, and he blamed me for this too. But I had another thing I could use. When I got my health back and men came to visit me, I told them that I was the fourth child born after three boys. None of the men wanted to marry me when they heard this because in my culture when a girl is born after three boys it is seen as very bad luck.

So all the proposals came to nothing. But my family were cleverer than me. They had been distributing my photograph around friends and relatives, and in 1994, when I was 23, a man came forward and proposed to my family that he wanted to marry me. I was very upset about this as I had made up my mind that I never wanted to marry, because I didn't have the blind faith of the rest of my family. They were supposed to be Buddhist but they still followed all the casteism and rituals of Hindu culture.

I tried everything I could to put this man off, but he still wanted to marry me. He invited me out to talk but I refused. Then one day a friend told me that he was a good man, a teacher, and that his mother had recently died so he had nobody to cook or clean for him. I felt sorry for him, and finally gave in to the pressure from my family. We got married, but I still felt insecure because I didn't love him, and I was still in love with the man from the different caste. I had seen him occasionally and still felt attracted to him. I felt dishonest and felt a need to tell my husband all about it. After I became pregnant with our first child I found the courage. I told him how my life had been before I met him, and to my surprise he supported me. He was angry with my father, and told me to see it as the past now and make the most of the future.

My husband was very good for me. He joined a young men's group that toured the villages giving lectures on Ambedkarism. Even when my father-in-law treated me badly, my husband stood by me. We lived harmoniously in the same house with my sister-in-law and her husband. But when her husband walked out, things began to change and my sister-in-law expected me to provide for her and her children. When I complained to my husband, my father-in-law beat me and told me to fulfil my duty as his daughter-in-law. We left the family home and set up home alone with our two children.

I don't regret my first love, and I know I am Lucky to have found an understanding husband. Many would have made me an outcaste if I'd told them I loved another man. Over time our relationship has developed and I can say I love him and feel very happy and fortunate.

Her mother died young
Education gave her strength
She dictates marriage

I was born Buddhist because my father was a Buddhist, but it didn't mean much when I was a child. It was just a piece of paper with the word 'Buddhist' stamped on it. I was told that my ancestors were once *Mahar* and now the family was Buddhist and that was all I needed to know.

I was born in Maharashtra in 1964 in an area where there are sugar cane factories. Many Dalits were employed by these factories and given living quarters as part of their wages. My father and many other people were illiterate, so school wasn't seen as a priority. In fact most of the children didn't go to school, they just played on the roads or on the rubbish heaps.

I belong to a family of four girls and two boys. My mother wasn't a strong woman. I remember her falling sick after the birth of each child, and six months after my youngest brother was born, she died. I remember this time very well. I was so sad when she died. When she was ill, I often used to wish that I could give her my life so she could continue to look after the family.

Three days before she died, she became unconscious and my uncle took her to the hospital several hours away. My oldest brother and sister were sent to my grandmother and the youngest were sent off to our uncle's. I refused to leave our home, because my mother was different from most parents living on the sugar cane plant. She said I must go to school, even though it was a 15-kilometre walk there and back. So I said I was going to stay at home with my father and walk to school every day. On the third day, I was in my maths class when a man came to my teacher and asked that I leave with him as my mother wanted to see me. I knew there was something strange about this, because she would never call me during school hours. She was always cross with my brothers and sisters and me if we were caught playing when we should have been at school. As I walked the 15 kilometres back, I knew my mother was dead, although the man was telling me she was looking forward to seeing me. When I arrived the whole family was there, and my worst fear came true. She was dead. The man hadn't told the truth and this had a terrible effect on me. I learned later that she had died from hepatitis.

This was the last time I saw her, as my father would not allow any of us to go to the funeral as he believed we were far too young. After this major event in my life, when I was 9, my father became depressed. He wasn't able to look after us well, and stopped mixing with friends. He also didn't know how to support us in education because he never went to school, but fortunately my mother's brother was educated, and encouraged him to keep sending us to school.

After a year all of us were sent away to live with different relatives because my father couldn't cope. I was sent to my father's mother's sister's house. In India she would be considered my grandmother too. Unfortunately she did not treat me very well. I was like a slave in her home. At six in the morning I would wake and have to work for four hours before attending school. My job was to clean the house, wash all the utensils and scrub the floor. I had to collect dung and roll it into balls for fuel, collect water from the well, and tend to the few cows they had in the field.

There was no security for me in this family. I felt my grandmother did not accept me, and I often felt bad about myself. She didn't like me to play, but this was confusing as I naturally wanted to play with the local children. One day she caught me, and from that day she began beating me. She wanted me just to work for her, and not play at all. After a few months I decided not to live there any more. My other brother and sisters were living elsewhere, and this gave me the courage to run away.

I went to my uncle because I knew he had supported my father and all of us children after our mother had died. It happened that there was a man visiting who suggested to my uncle that he take me to a hostel for poor Dalit children. They would feed me and give me education, and in return I would work on their farm and do cleaning work. My brother agreed, and my life changed from that moment. I began to feel good about myself and made some nice friends, and the adults working there were very caring. The hostel had about 80 children and only seven of us were girls. It was unusual in the 1970s in my community to allow girls to have education. However the teachers encouraged all of us very much, though we often got teased by the boys, and they would play tricks on us, like putting dung on our chairs. One of the teachers really liked me, and when I was 11 years old, he suggested I try for the high school that the charity ran. There was a hostel for girls there; the girls lived downstairs and the high school was upstairs. He believed in my intelligence and told me that this was my only way out of my poverty and family suffering.

My younger sister joined me when I was in the second year, so it was a good experience for me. My father was able to keep paying for our education as he only had to pay a nominal fee. However, when I was 12, my mother's father tried to marry me off. When I came home for a school holiday, he sat me down and said: "There are people coming to see you. If you marry one of these men now, it will make it easier for me to marry your two younger sisters. If you stay in education, they will have a problem." I just sat and stared at the floor, I didn't say anything. And then I began to cry, and I told my grandmother that I didn't want to marry, I wanted to study. For two days I refused to eat, and when the prospective men came round to see me, I refused to go and stand in front of them. This caused a major problem in the family but in the end my uncle agreed to support my education. So this gave me a confidence boost.

I was very successful at school. I managed to pass my 10th standard exam, and my father agreed that I could stay at the hostel and continue my education at college. However, my mother's parents had different ideas. I was 16 and they wanted me married. They tried again, but this time I was older and I could stand up to them. I had some power too, because I got excellent marks in my exams, and the hostel charity agreed to pay for all my education, my books, and travel to college. So it would cost my family nothing.

My grandfather refused to speak to me after I turned down his request, and instead he found a husband for my next youngest sister, who was 15 at the time. Unlike me, she was not able to put up a fight; she had very little confidence. I was determined to continue with my education. I wanted to be a doctor, because I had been inspired by doctors at a young age, and was still angry that my mother hadn't been given the right medicine when she was sick.

I remember when I was about six I caught scabies, and my father took me to the hospital and said: "You must be really good, because when you go inside, there will be a god there." After this god saw me, I got rid of my scabies, and I also remembered that there were many people waiting to see the god. I was inspired that somebody could make people well and help to save people's lives. So after my mother died, I vowed I would become a doctor.

I moved to the city and was admitted into a college to do sciences. I was supported by a scholarship so this was manageable. I was teased a lot, as there were very few Dalits at this college and very few women learning the sciences. Everyone knew I was poor and a Dalit because I only had two saris and I wore them in the village way, hitched up between my legs. Most of the students were fashionable and wore Western clothes. But I was able to stand my ground, and my uncle continued to donate some money towards my education, so I could buy a few more things for myself.

When I completed two years of science, I was admitted to a six-year doctors' training course in aryuvedic and allopathic medicines. Since I was a distinction student from the Dalit community, I was given all my living expenses, plus money for books and travel. However, my grandparents still weren't happy. Halfway through my course, when I was 22, they insisted I marry and began to put immense pressure on me. Their argument was that they had enough money now to pay a dowry for me and my youngest sister, and so they wanted to marry us both off now. It was a final decision. I had to marry. I tried to argue that I wanted the right to choose the man. Why was it that the man comes to see the girl and then decides if he will marry her? Why couldn't I have some say in it if I had to live with him for the rest of my life? But they wouldn't listen.

I found out that the man who had been invited to look at me was a doctor, and so I set about finding out where he worked. When I found out, I decided to pay him a visit. I turned up at his workplace and said: "You are coming to look at me tomorrow with a view to marriage. But if you want to marry me, you must first agree to my conditions. You can marry me, but I will not come to live with you immediately. First I want my degree, so I will marry you but continue to live in the hostel for the next three years. If you are agreeable to this, then please come to my family home tomorrow. If not, don't bother to come at all." He just laughed in my face. But I was satisfied, and returned to my home. I knew that if I went to live with him straight after my marriage, that would be the end of my studies. I would be serving his family and having babies.

The next day, to my surprise he came with his relatives. He agreed to marry me and didn't say a word to anybody about my visit. So I was able to complete my education, and after I graduated as a doctor I went to live with him. I am fortunate. I like him, and although our thoughts may not be the same, we get on well. We have one beautiful daughter and she is brought up differently from the way I was. We both decided that one child was enough if we were to give her the best opportunities in life. It was better to focus on one child than to try to spread our income among three. And we've had no pressure from our families. I've been fortunate to fulfil my vision. At the age of 25 I began working as a doctor in a private practice. My husband and I have been able to buy a house, a car, nice furniture and all the material things I dreamed of as a child.

However, I still felt empty. My needs weren't being met. I realised there was more to life than money, and money couldn't make me happy. So I began to get involved with social work, through visiting some of the hostels in the community. It was a way of giving back to the system that I grew up in. Because of the hostels I was able to change my life; they gave me so much. Some of the hostels were different from the ones I grew up in. They were in the slums, and this made me aware of another life. I realised I wanted to work for the poor, the people who really needed my help. The hostel charity I grew up in was called the Saint Gadge Maharaj Mission. It was named after a man who wanted to serve all the needy and poor people in society, and provide them with clean and supportive surroundings. I was inspired by this saint.

Since then, the direction of my life has changed. I am 41, and still happily married. I work as a doctor and counsellor for the Bahujan Hitay medical project in Pimpri slums. The main problem is the issue of child marriage. So many people in India who live in the slums and villages believe that as soon as a girl begins her menstruation they must stop her education and keep her imprisoned in the family house till a husband has been found. The parents are afraid of premarital pregnancy and affairs. If the girls are confident they can protest and manage to convince their parents to allow them to continue their education. But such girls are few.

It means that we have a high percentage of child marriage happening at 11, 12 and 13. Marriage has a huge effect on a girl this young. She is unable to accept her responsibilities as a wife and mother. She finds it hard to accept her newborn, and often these babies are born underweight and extremely anaemic. It is impossible for girls of this age to be physically, emotionally and spiritually prepared for such a major event in any woman's life. Child marriage destroys a young girl's body and puts her babies at risk too. Also, because so many of our girls are giving birth so young, their span for child-bearing is 30 or more years, and that inevitably has a huge impact on the increase of population, which is something India is struggling with.

So part of my work is trying to educate the young Dalit women and their parents to do something different. And this includes all of us, Hindu, Muslim, Christian and Buddhist. The Dalit women of all religions who live in the villages and the slums are still suffering. The facilities in slum areas are still minimal, so we are still faced with illnesses like typhoid, malaria, hepatitis and leprosy. HIV is an even bigger problem, because in Indian culture women do not openly talk about sex, so it is very hard to pick it up before it is too late. It's the men who pass it on to the women, but it is the women who lose out.

If the husband finds out his wife has the AIDS virus, despite the fact that he has it too, he will abandon her, and move on to another woman. Recently I was working with a young woman who contracted the virus and was too scared to admit it to anybody. Finally, the hospital made it clear to her husband what was happening and insisted he be tested. The wife died and he ran off, abandoning four young children. Not being able to talk about these things also makes it difficult for us to work with the increase of rape and sexual abuse in the family. So my job as a doctor is much more than writing prescriptions and giving medicines. It's about social work and the development of my community. It is necessary to perform this double duty. Much has to be done in India to change the lives of women. I am only working at the surface. We need money to support our projects if we are to make any long-term changes.

> *A dowry burning*
> *Not news in the media*
> *It's my family*

There are three girls in my family. My eldest sister married in 1977 when I was 8 years old. I couldn't understand what was wrong with her, because she was not happy when her proposal was arranged. I heard our father say: "If you don't marry I will die." My mother said: "You have to marry. Think about your younger sisters." I heard all these things and saw she was afraid. She tried to explain to me that she didn't want to marry because the man had no job and wasn't educated. She told me that our parents only wanted her to marry him because he was the only son in his family. My sister gave in to the pressure and married him when she was 16.

Her husband began beating her for small things, but my mother and father wouldn't give her permission to return home. They said: "You must go back to his house even if he beats you so badly you die there." I even remember the neighbours saying to my sister: "Why have you come back here? Marriage is very important. You must stay with your husband whatever happens."

My sister couldn't live with the abuse and left her husband without consulting my parents. She went to a lady who had no children herself and treated my sister like her own child. This lady gave her emotional support, and allowed her to stay for as long as she liked. She taught my sister to fend for herself, by teaching her the trade of sewing. My parents left her alone during the first year because she was out of sight of all the neighbours and her husband never came and complained. My sister seemed to be happy there; she was smiling again when she visited. She even got a job and tried to be independent because she had to bring money home for my parents.

But my mother and father began blaming the lady for taking their daughter away from her husband, and one day when my sister came to bring us money they wouldn't give her permission to return. They said: "Go back to your husband's house. If you stay with that lady, who will marry your sisters?" My brother began to put pressure on her as well. She left the house unhappy and never came back to visit.

And so, after almost two years of living with the lady, she was forced to go back to her husband's house. She told me and my other sister: "I have no other way, so I have to learn to compromise because our father will not give me permission to stay with you, and he won't let me stay with the lady." At a meeting in our house, her husband said: "You come. I'll take you back, it will be different now." But it was obvious that he was just going to beat her again. This man's nature was so bad that even his mother wasn't living with him, which was unusual. I saw how he beat my sister so cruelly. She would sometimes come to the house with blood dripping down her face, but still my parents didn't do anything. I witnessed all these things as a child. I saw all these things.

He began to lock her up in their house every time he left it, so when we went to see her we had to speak to her through a small window. I could see that my mother did begin to feel sad, but my father said: "It's better you stay with him, and maybe he will slowly change." Things did change. She gave birth to three children who are now adults, but he still continued to maltreat her. I may have been young when this happened but it had a big effect on me. People thought that I was too young to realise what was happening, but it was on my mind all the time. I was very angry with my father. My sister is a family member, so why did he not look after her? Why did he treat her like this? But as I've grown up, I've learned that the culture I live in is to blame. In India when a girl marries she must stay with her husband no matter what.

My second sister's situation was quite different. She was the eldest in her in-laws' family, because her husband was the eldest in the family. This meant they both had responsibility for looking after the family. She was married at 18. A relative found the proposal. The relative only knew the man's mother and we soon learned that we had been cheated. His mother was a Buddhist and had married a Jain. They cheated us because we didn't know this was an inter-caste marriage. We discovered at the engagement ceremony that the whole family were Jains except for the mother, who is Buddhist.

My mother was shocked when she found out that it was an inter-caste marriage. It wasn't my sister's fault, but they had invited all the guests to the party so they had to go ahead. Other relatives said: "Just go ahead. If this marriage is cancelled, people will blame your daughter, and if people know that her first marriage didn't happen, they will not turn up at her next engagement ceremony." My mother was so worried about this that in the end she gave in. Unfortunately, my sister's new family didn't treat her very well. She was made to do all the work and they didn't give her enough food to eat. They treated her as if she was an 'Untouchable'. My sister was the most beautiful one in the family but when she married and went to that family she became weak and looked sick. After two years of marriage, she gave birth to a daughter. Because the baby was a girl, nobody was happy and nobody went to see her in the hospital. From that time, difficulties arose.

When I was 16, one morning before school, my brother was shouting at me, telling me that I had to study hard and concentrate. I left home without saying goodbye and went to my neighbours' house. Later that day when I came back from school my brother and mother were both crying and I said: "Why are you crying? Is it because I didn't listen to you this morning?" and my mother said: "No, your sister has been burned." I was shocked by this news.

Three days before she was burned, she came to our house and complained that her in-laws were demanding money, and telling her to go to her mother's house and find something to bring back for them. The in-laws' family were thinking that as this was the Diwali vacation, they could get things from my mother. My mother said: "I will give you a letter to say I have nothing." I also remember saying to my sister: "Why don't you be strong? Why don't you tell them our mother's house is not very rich?" She replied: "I did tell them that, but they won't listen to me." She came again the next day and again began demanding that we give her something. I told her: "Why don't you say to them we have nothing to give? We don't have enough food for ourselves. Tell them their demands are too big." After I heard that she had been burned, I felt very guilty.

When we arrived at the hospital, someone took us aside and told us that some of the hospital staff had heard her husband threatening her: "If the police come to take a statement and you say anything, remember you only have one brother." The nurses reported this to my family but were not prepared to be witnesses for fear of losing their jobs and being persecuted. She was my mother's most beautiful daughter, and when I went to the hospital I saw that she was burned from head to toe. She could only say a few sentences: "When I am well I want to come to mother's house. I don't want to go back there." But there was no chance for her to live because she had 99 per cent first degree burns. Her skin was hanging off her. She died four hours later.

My eldest sister went immediately to the in-laws' house when she heard, to find out exactly what happened. She wanted to see for herself how our sister died. It was suspicious because only one side of the house was burned, and the neighbours told her that when the house was burning, pouring with smoke, family members just went outside to the common toilet, and someone went to and came back from the shop as if nothing was happening. There were no screams, and no voices shouting for help. Only when they saw the black smoke did people begin to run out of the house.

Despite all this evidence there was no means for my family to get help. The in-laws had reported to the police that it was suicide. They had given a statement before we reached the police station. The police told us there was no case, because it was clear that it was suicide. We couldn't fight the verdict because in India once a girl is married she becomes the property of her husband's family. When my sister was burned, the in-laws immediately hid all the proof of her murder. We found out that they gave money to the police and to some local political people to cover up her death and make it look like suicide.

Because I was 16, nobody wanted to speak to me about this, because they assumed I was still a child. Nobody listened to my opinion or asked how I was. I had read about dowry burning murders in the newspapers, but I saw this atrocity in my own family. I decided from that moment that I didn't want to marry. But this is India. I would have to marry one day. I hated the thought of the married life. I didn't want to marry, but I knew I must pass my exams to avoid marriage. I failed, but my parents let me take them again and that time I passed. They decided to leave me alone. After that year my life changed. From this time my mother died inside her heart. She became mad, talking to my sister in her sleep. We worried about her mental state.

I went to the Ambedkar college, and at the same time I heard about Buddhism from a monk friend I met at college. He took me to lectures. I lost interest in my studies and became more interested in Ambedkar and meditation. When I meditated it was the only time I felt some peace and happiness after my sister's death. I had many painful stories in my heart, and it was a good place to express myself and my grief. I didn't want to lose this opportunity. So I concentrated on meditation and *Dhamma* study, and began to forget my other studies.

My parents began to shout at me. They were very upset about my two sisters' marriages, so they didn't force me to marry. They said: "You study and don't worry. We won't marry you now." But I couldn't study because I had found inner peace by meditating. My brother and my father began to get angry with me, and told me that meditation is work for older people. Young people shouldn't be chanting and worshipping gods. I began to miss my lectures and didn't attend college. My brother shouted at me even more: "If you're not going to study, we will marry you." So this became dangerous for me. I told them that I didn't want marriage and I wasn't interested in study either.

They stopped all my expenses, so I began to earn pocket money by giving tuition to children so I could attend retreats. But they didn't listen to me and began to look for a marriage proposal for me. When I was 19 my brother got very angry with me because I was becoming too involved with Buddhism. One day, I went to a talk at a TBMSG centre, and when I returned, he had locked me out. I banged on the door but he wouldn't open up. I had to go back to the centre and ask one of the men to come back with me to ask my parents to let me into the house. This was successful. My brother opened the door, and shouted at the man telling him he was crazy and the Buddhists were making me crazy. While he was cursing him, I entered the house without him even noticing me. But when he shut the door he came and found me and beat me.

I heard from the TBMSG group that there was an opening for a community member to live and work at a girls' hostel in Pune. I asked my parents if I could go to Pune to meditate, study and help the poor children, but they said no, I had to continue my education and find a good job. But I told them that this was where I wanted to go. They didn't give me permission. Instead they found a proposal for me. He was a man living alone. He had no family members and was very educated, an engineer, and so my parents were very happy. They thought I was very lucky, and that I should be happy about this.

When I found out about this man, I began to plan to run away. I collected my money, one bed sheet, three dresses and a small bag, and wrote a letter to my parents, and very silently and carefully gave my bag to my friend when nobody was in my house, and told her to take it and go to the main road and wait for me. In the letter I wrote: "I'm making my own decision. Don't come after me and don't bring me back here. I will come and see you again, but now I'm leaving for Pune, and this is my responsibility." I didn't give them my address as I didn't even know it myself. I only knew what district the hostel was in. I didn't even know which train station I had to go to. It was the first time I had travelled on the express train.

I arrived in Pune, and I asked many people where there was a girls' hostel in the district, and eventually somebody knew where it was. My family didn't come after me immediately, but I know they shouted at the TBMSG people, and blamed them for taking their daughter away and teaching me bad ways. When the TBMSG people found out that I had left my home without my parents' permission, they weren't so friendly to me. They didn't want to accept me, but they let me stay there. They didn't think I would last long. Some people just said: "She's a Bombay girl, she look likes a town girl, how will she be able to do hostel work? She won't last." They also said: "She looks like a student. How can she help the other students?" But I was determined to stay. I decided that when they accepted me I would go and see my family.

My brother did track me down, but I refused to see him. I agreed to meet his wife. I told her: "I'm not coming. You just tell him not to worry because it's my decision." Meanwhile my, brother met the hostel workers and the people told him not to worry, they would take care of me. I heard that he was also shown around the place, and he left, and was satisfied that the place was safe.

After this, the community accepted me, now that my family were satisfied. I became an assistant warden, and after a couple of years I became the warden, which was a big job, taking care of the children and their education, their parents and the caretakers. I lived in the hostel with a community of eleven women. Not all of us worked at the hostel, but we all practised daily meditation and *Dhamma* study and I knew I had made the best decision. It was a very enjoyable life. I got good energy from the work, and I learned how to do casework with the students.

My parents began to worry because I was 24 by then. They said: "Come home. You have to marry." My mother was very sick and worried. Since my sister's death, she had declined and was now confined to her bed. Plus, my brother's first wife had left him, so there was nobody to look after her. So I decided I had to go back home to take care of my mother. It was a major decision. My brother began to put more pressure on me, and I knew the time had come when I must marry.

My mother would say: "Your brother has remarried and he's settled again, and your eldest sister is settled. When you are married, I will be happy to die. When you sleep, you just think about marriage." She was so ill that her words affected me. All the members of my family shouted at me saying: "Why aren't you listening? She won't die till you marry." So one day I said to a person I had met before I moved to Pune: "My mother is thinking about my marriage, but who will marry me at my age?" He took this opportunity and said: "I would like to marry you. I have always liked you." So I said: "I must ask my family first."

So I married without thinking. I did it out of duty to my mother. Seven months later she died. My mother was my inspiration. She was the only person who knew about Buddhism in my family. And I know she was secretly pleased with my life. She was an uneducated, illiterate person, but she could speak more than six of the languages which exist in India.

I know that the experience of my two sisters' marriages have affected my relationship with men. Fortunately I have a beautiful daughter, and my husband is kind to me, does not beat me, and allows me to live an independent life. I'm away from home a lot, visiting rural villages and teaching the women about Buddhism, Ambedkar and their rights in today's society. I realise that we women need to be strong. I'm not saying men are bad; it's their attitudes which are negative. The situation of marriage in India is our society's problem. We have to change our attitudes to the marriage of our daughters.

Some are strong
Married, divorced, single
They are all cursed

I grew up in a Dalit community where most of the people were very poor. I lived a Hindu life, worshipping the gods and visiting *sadhus*, and we were treated as the lowest of the low by the Brahmins, so there was really no escape from the Hindu culture for us. Most of my community worked in the fields all day for very little money. Our houses were dilapidated, and people didn't have many clothes. My family was slightly different because my father worked for ex-servicemen and earned good wages, so I began life living quite well with proper clothes on my back and enough food to eat. But by the time I was five or six my father had become addicted to gambling. He would be away working for the whole month and return with no wages. Sometimes he would not return when he was expected and my mother had to go in search of him. So we became like all the other Dalit families in the village, extremely poor, because he never brought any money home. We started off with six children in my family, but three of them died because we didn't have enough money for medicine. One of my sisters also died because her husband didn't treat her properly. After she gave birth to her first child, she died of typhoid because he neglected and abused her.

My marriage to my husband was not successful either. He was not good to me, and we lived in great poverty. During this time my mother died. In fact, between 1966 and 1975, three of my siblings and my parents all died. I was ten when my family began dying and 19 by the time the last one died. My father died of a broken heart when I was 15 because he was so upset by the failure of my eldest sister's marriage, and my mother died shortly after. This left my youngest sister and brother, and I was not in a position to look after them because of my husband's temperament, so they went to live with their grandmother. I felt ashamed because my brother, who was only seven at the time, had run away from my house because my husband was beating me, but in the end I knew it was for the best. My sister was sent to our aunt's, but this was traumatic for her too. Our aunt treated my sister badly. She didn't send her to school, but kept her at home so she could work in the house for her, and help out in the fields and work as a labourer. It was a very hard time for us all.

When I was 25 I gave birth to a son, and I hoped this would make my husband happy. But it didn't change his ways, and when we moved to another backward village he became worse. He doubted me, didn't let me speak to other people in the village and kept me locked up in the house unless I went out to work with him in the fields. He accused me of sleeping with other men, and gave me no comfort. And then he decided to stop working, so I began collecting vegetables and selling them from the roadside. I had to take my son and go out to work; I used to lay him down beside the vegetables and fruit so I could earn money for my family.

With all these pressures on me, I was unable to look after my child properly, and one day he died. After our son died at ten months of age, I hoped that my husband would change, that he would feel sad, but nothing changed. So I found the courage to leave. I told him: "I can't stay any more." He didn't want this at all, and he didn't believe I would go. But I took my chance of freedom and left. I got my divorce and went to live with my sister and brother, who were both in their teens.

We had dreamed of living back in our family house which our mother had left. But when we returned, the village people had ransacked it, destroyed it completely. So with the small pension that was left we rented a small place and I went out to work so that my sister could have some education. My brother was 16 and old enough to work, but because I was divorced and a single woman he began to treat me differently. He began demanding money from me. I was working in a kindergarten during the day, making plastic garlands to sell at the weekend, and sewing garments for ladies at night to help keep the house. But my brother decided he was the boss of the house because he was the man, and he wanted to make all the decisions about the money I was earning. I wouldn't give anything to him, so he would often come and find my money and take it.

At the same time I tried to educate myself. I only went to school until I was 8. I had to help my parents work in the fields, and often they told me not to go to school because they needed money. After working in the fields, at the age of 15 I became a labourer, working on the streets, digging trenches in the roads, chopping rocks, mixing clay and carrying it on my head for the men to make new roads. And then I married at 18. So there was no time to study.

I needed more money for my studies, so I managed to find a job as a cleaner in a government hospital. There weren't many women working there and I was often disrespected because I was a single woman in my mid 20s. One man tried to have sex with me, but I managed to fight him off. It was distressing; men thought it was their right to harass me because I was divorced. I had seen many men be abusive to other single and divorced women too. When you live alone without a husband they feel it's their right to have sex with you.

But working in the hospital gave me some freedom. It was a long journey from home, but I managed to do three shifts and save a little. My brother became frustrated because he couldn't have as much control over me as he wished. So one day he followed me to work and on my long journey home, he came up to me with three of his friends and demanded Rs. 2,000 from me. He said: "If you don't give me the money, I will kill you." One of his friends stood and waved a knife in front of my face. So I had to give him all the money I had on me. The next day, when I returned home he had locked me out, and he said I could only come back into the house if I handed all my money over. He thought he had a right to treat me like this because I was a divorced woman. Since I was single he felt I should be totally dependent on him. He hated my independence. To protect myself from this harassment I went to the train station and slept in the waiting room. I did this for several weeks. I also found out I could keep money in a bank account. This was good because I was able to secretly save money and buy a small house for my sister and me.

Working in the hospital allowed me to free myself from my brother. I was promoted and began to earn more money. I suddenly had more money than I had ever dreamed of. I was proud; I had always wanted money because I knew it was power. But soon I felt sad, and realised that although I had independence, as a single woman in India, which was unusual for women from the Dalit caste, I wasn't happy. Fortunately, I came across an interesting Sri Lankan monk, and he was offering something different. He wasn't offering money. He was offering peace of mind through meditation and Buddhist teachings. It all began to make sense for me, and then I began to become interested in the social movement for women. I realised that I was driven by greed, and needed to purify this and begin to work for the benefit of others as well as myself. I came across Dr. Ambedkar and was inspired by his thinking. I couldn't believe it when I read that he wanted social uplift for both men and women, that he wanted girls as well as boys to be educated.

I have left my hospital work and have become involved with Non-Government Organisations funded by the Karuna Trust in England, working solely for the improvement and equality of women. I am trying to help women become aware of themselves and how they can begin to change their lives. I am trying to help dismantle a whole Indian tradition. In my culture it is a woman's nature to be servile. Women think they can't do anything, and stay cooped up in their houses. They believe they have to remain dependent on their husbands no matter what and let them make all the decisions. Too many women in India are too scared to leave their abusive husbands. Their attitude is: "We can't get up and leave. How can we go outside alone and live on our own?" I am trying to help women see differently. I managed it, and it is possible for them to manage it too.

Today I'm in my 40s, but my brother still feels it's his right to control me because I'm not married. He only calls me when he needs money and expects me to give it to him. But I stand my ground. My money is for the uplift of Dalit women.

Village Life

Proud Dalit lady
Chapatti rises in flames
Chief of her village

I was elected the leader of the village, the Sarapanch, in 2005. This means that I am the head of the village council, the Panchayat. I am the first Dalit woman in my district since the independence of India ever to hold such a prestigious position. It happened because it was the turn of the Backward Community to have an opportunity to run for leadership. This time reservations (positive discrimination, opportunities for Dalit women to run for election) were applied to my village, and I had the chance of running for leadership in my village. I had never thought about being a politician or holding such a position, but when the reservations opportunity came to my village, the people encouraged me to stand, because they believed I was trustworthy and would not be influenced by corruption. They said that my family was always kind and generous and willing to help anybody with their difficulties, and because there was a roster for a person from a Scheduled Caste to stand for this position, it should be me.

I won more votes than any other person who has run for leadership in the past 25 years, which came as a huge surprise. I feel very happy to have the opportunity to serve my society effectively. The total population of the village is 3,000 people, from about 450 families. Fifty per cent of us are from the Dalit communities and tribal communities and the other 50 per cent are Brahmins and other high caste people. Of course there is tension between the castes. This is the reality of India, but during my first year there has been great peace between all of us.

My village provides education up to the age of 12, run by the council, and there is a small private high school for children up to the age of 16. It is mainly the Brahmins and other caste Hindus who attend the high school as most Dalit families cannot afford the fees. Most of the Dalits do farming and labouring for the Brahmins and other high caste Hindus who own the land, but they do, on the whole, pay reasonable wages. Most of the time my village lives in harmony. The percentage of literate people is higher than that of the other villages nearby, and the Dalit community are mainly Ambedkarites, which means their minds aren't riddled with superstitions or dependent on gods.

I am responsible for the schools, local needs and facilities. The whole village is my responsibility. I will be in office for five years. During my time I hope to build proper roads, provide proper drainage for sewage and invest in many social welfare projects. Dear to my heart is the issue of making the village free from people defecating in the streets. By the time my term comes to an end I would like to see a toilet in every house. A person going to the toilet anywhere in the village creates an unhealthy environment for everyone. Already I have managed to raise Rs. 12,000 ($300) from the state government. I am also trying to care for the people who are below the poverty line as there are many people in my village who are too poor to feed their children. I would also like to form groups for women where they can come together and help each other get loans from the bank. There is proof that our women are much more capable than men of looking after money and saving. I have a very big task ahead of me, as there are many problems in the village. One of the biggest is domestic violence. This is extremely tricky. Domestic disputes are very delicate to get involved with, as they are considered family matters, and nobody else's business. So it is incredibly difficult to help the many women and children who are at risk.

Since becoming a leader, I have been mixing closely with high caste Hindus for the first time in my life. But they all seem to respect me. In fact they have no choice. I must say that I've not experienced any discrimination to my face, but I don't know if discrimination goes on in their minds. I am beginning to enjoy the life of politics; it's the first time in my life I've been able to put my views across. On Independence Day and Republic Day I am invited to go out in public and hoist the national flag. Whoever is the head of the village has the right to raise the flag ceremoniously on these days. This is a great honour for a Dalit woman. I feel proud to represent my country, proud that I have the opportunity to conduct this ceremony. Who would have believed 50 years ago that a Dalit, a Backward Class, a Scheduled Class, an ex 'Untouchable', a woman, would be raising the flag of India?

I must admit that I live in the neighbouring town, although I visit the village every day. This is because once my children became ten, I wanted them to have a suitable education. I prefer the countryside and my connections with people in the village, but I have to think of the long-term needs of my children. Part of my children's education is paid for by scholarships; also, my husband owns a farm and distributes gas bottles to all the local villages, and I receive a nominal fee for my work with the council. I want my son and daughter to have a different life from me and my husband, and I especially want my daughter to have more opportunities and freedom.

I was born in a village called Sukali. I have three sisters and one brother. My parents brought all five of us up but they were very poor. My father was a bus conductor on a state bus. He was only educated up to the age of 14. And my mother went to school till the age of 12. After that she was married off quite soon. It was mainly Scheduled Caste people in my village, so prejudice against us didn't seem to be a big problem, though of course it did happen. Education wasn't a priority, but I was allowed to go to school till the age of 16. I wanted to continue my studies but my father insisted it was time I was married. He wanted all four girls off his hands as soon as possible, so he found a husband for each of us as soon as he could. So I was married at the age of 16. It was arranged by my parents. I didn't know anything at this age. I didn't have the maturity to understand what marriage was about. It was something that happened and I had to get used to it. Although I am happy now, it was extremely traumatic. I will not allow my daughter to have that experience. I will encourage her to take the opportunity of a higher education, and will not allow her to marry early.

I have brought my children up to know about Ambedkar and understand what it means to be a Dalit in this society. I hope this will influence their choices, and that they too will want to do something for their community. My leadership is greatly influenced by Dr. Ambedkar's philosophy. My grandmother taught me about him when I was a child. Although she couldn't read or write, she told me all about Dr. Ambedkar's life, often before I went to bed. She recited from his book, *The Buddha and His Dhamma*, to me, and told me about all the struggles and hardships of the Dalit people. My grandmother reminded me daily that I was a Buddhist, and I feel very proud to have this religion. I am proud of my country, my ancestry and cultural background. Too many people from Dalit backgrounds are forgetting their history. They live in the city, earn a lot of money and then conceal their Buddhist side, because they want the full respect of the Brahmins and the other high caste Hindus. I could never live like that. I want to live openly, and I want to teach my children that it is all right to be a Buddhist in India. I am not afraid of calling myself an Ambedkarite. Although my parents were poor, I'm proud of who I am. I refuse to hide my Dalit roots. There is no need to pretend that you come from a higher caste. How can people live like that? Dalit people must live the Buddhist way with confidence. I hope that I am a role model for the people in my village, and that they can feel proud of their Ambedkarite roots.

> *Village life is hard*
> *In rice fields under the sun*
> *70 pence a day*

From the age of 11 I began to work in the fields. I had to help bring money back for the home. My mother died when I was 7 and I had two younger sisters and two older brothers so I had to stay at home to raise them. All of us were working from the age of seven because there was never enough money. We worked in the rice fields and when some of us were 14, we could do labouring work. I come from a poor Hindu village and my childhood was poor, and I believe this is the case in many villages in India.

My father and brother arranged my marriage when I was 18, because they needed to be able to marry my younger sisters, and so I began providing for my in-laws. I worked so hard that I lost my first baby to a miscarriage. Nobody was there to help me when I lost my child in the fields. I felt very nervous. I have three beautiful children now, but my life is still troubled. I am 32, and living in my husband's village, which is even poorer than the one I grew up in. We're all Hindus of all castes, and we are all poor. There is no high school here, and my children have to walk for more than 90 minutes for their education. I have to pay their fees, along with medical fees for my second son, who is ill because he didn't receive a vaccination when he was born.

I make a great effort so that my children can live a good life, but I am only paid Rs. 60 a day in the fields, although my husband is paid Rs. 80 for the same work. There is no other work for those of us who live in the village, and I am afraid that my children will end up having to do the same work. Working in the fields is harsh. It's impossible to enjoy it. I have to wake up early and work all day under the fierce sun in the rice or wheat fields, and when I come home at 4, I have to take care of the home. I am worried for my daughter. It is dangerous for young women to work in the fields because so many of them are raped and sexually exploited. I want her to have a good education, but I know I won't be able to afford to keep her at school after she is 14, because the books and fees cost too much. I worry about my children's future. I don't want them to suffer like me, but it is impossible to earn any more.'

If my children are able to be educated, this will make me happy. If they get good jobs, this will make me happy. What more can I do? My responsibility is too much. My time is busy with working and looking after the children, and my husband, and my in-laws. This is the life in the village: not much hope for the new generation, and not enough money to give them an education that will give them independence from this life.

> *I'm a town girl now*
> *My family - village slaves*
> *Back turns on this life*

I was born in 1983 in a Hindu village in Maharashtra. I am the eldest of four children; I have two brothers and one sister. My parents' economic situation is very bad. I had another brother who was born before me, but because of my parents' poverty he died when he was just a few months old. There was very little food in the home, so when I was born my grandparents came to my parents' village and took me to the town to live with them.

My father works on land matters. He collects information about the village, and records the births and deaths. He is called a Patwari, a government representative. His wage is very low, and so, when the third child was born, my grandparents collected him from the village too. We grew up differently from our younger brother and sister, because when they were born, my parents felt they could afford to look after them.

My grandparents are like my own parents. They are much better off than my parents. My grandfather still has a very good job in the government. He is a district officer. They were determined that my brother and I would have a good education and not end up like our mother, who married someone with no education or work. My whole family is from the Scheduled Caste; we are *Matangs*. The *Matangs* are more backward than the *Mahars*. We have not converted to Buddhism; we are still Hindus. There are a few of us who are educated and in good government jobs, unlike the ex-*Mahar* people, who are more successful. In my parents' village we still carry dead bodies and dead animals for the Brahmins and high caste Hindus. If we don't do this work, the Panchayat (village council) takes action against us. My parents' village is a mixture of *Matangs* and high caste people like the Brahmin and Maratha people. But it's the Brahmins who control the Panchayat and the whole village. In the town where I still live with my grandparents, there are *Matangs* and Brahmins, but there is very little discrimination. I have faced very little prejudice at school, at college and in the town.

However, visiting my parents' village every school holidays was another story. Every year in the summer holidays my brother and I travelled over two hours to our parents' village. After one or two days, I wanted to go back home. I only wanted to be a guest in my parents' home. I would ring my grandparents and beg them to come and collect me. But they told me I had to stay with my parents so I could get to know them properly. I didn't like the atmosphere there because my father drank all day and then quarrelled with my mother, and my younger sister refused to speak to me. My mother didn't know how to cope with my father or the conflict between me and my sister. Often she would scream: "I think it would be better for you to go back to your grandparents."

I hated all the superstition and worship of gods in the village. I could see how my sister was growing up to be a passive Hindu woman. She has been taught to bathe before she touches any food or attends any rituals. She believes that she is only pure when she has a bath. She has learned to worship the god Ganpati, also known as Ganesh. He has a body like a human and a face like an elephant, has four hands and is said to travel with a mouse.

The story goes like this. A Hindu god called Shankar was married to Parvati. One day when Parvati was going to bathe, Shankar was not at home. She thought: "Who is going to guard me and my home while I take this bath?" She sat and thought about this for a while, and then an idea arose in her mind. She took her clothes off in secret and then took all the dust and dirt from her body, and from this dirt she made a human body and put it in front of the door as a guard. She then relaxed and took her bath. But while she was enjoying her bath, her husband, Shankar, returned. He was shocked. Why was there a soldier guarding his door? He tried to walk past the statue but as he tried to enter his home, the statue spoke: "Do not go inside this house." Shankar was furious. How dare someone forbid him entry to his own home? So he took his sword and screamed: "Who are you to tell me I can't enter my own home?" and beheaded the guard with one blow. Parvati cried out, and Shankar ran in to see what had happened. To his surprise his wife was angry with him. She was disappointed and cried for her guard; she wanted him back. So Shankar apologised and said he would only return when he had found a head for the guard. He went to the jungle and chopped off the head of the first animal he saw, which was an elephant, and came back and placed the elephant's head on top of the statue.

Because of this story women are seen as unclean. Ganpati is worshipped by many in my parents' village. People bring sweets and wheat grass and leave them at his feet. They pray to him in the hope of becoming wealthy. They ask him to rid them of their difficulties. This is just one of the many gods and goddesses that my parents and younger brother and sister worship.

I also hated it in the village because all of a sudden I felt inferior, as if there was something wrong with me. If I took my younger sister to the *balwadi* (kindergarten) I would have to stand in one line with *Matangs* while the higher caste people stood in another line. When there were wedding ceremonies, all the *Matang* people had to sit at the back and watch the others eat all the good food. When they finished, the Brahmins would call us to eat the leftovers. I began to refuse to go to these village events and my parents were angry with me.

In the hot summer the well, would often dry out, and the little water there was always had dust in it. When my parents or other *Matang* families went to complain to the Panchayat and ask what they could do, saying: "If there is no water all our families will die," the Panchayat just laughed and told them to go to another well. They had their own private water for themselves. Often, the whole of my family along with many other *Matangs* would walk over an hour to the next village for water. But the Brahmin people there refused to let us draw water, so we would have to sleep in the bushes at night and in the early morning steal the water. Once, many of us were caught and there was a big fight, and they threatened to call the police, so we had to leave all our water behind and flee.

When my father tries to do his job, many of the high caste people do not welcome him warmly and their children refer to him in a condescending and undermining way, as if they are better than him. They speak to him rudely. In Hindu culture children are supposed to respect their elders, but when it comes to Dalits, the high caste children have no respect for us. These injustices are still happening in my parents' village. I'm not an old person; I have just completed my 23rd year. So I am worried for my young brother and sister. My brother is 16 now, and he is very clever, but the Brahmins will not give him good marks. All the *Matangs* who go to the school an hour away from the village suffer from this persecution. Brahmin teachers refuse to mark them higher than the Brahmin children. I would like to have enough money to bring my brother to the city where I live, so he can get the educational opportunities he deserves. My father has been careless with his salary and at times does not turn up at work, so it's not possible for him to support my brother's education. He didn't have to worry about my sister as she is a female and her husband will look after her. She is 19 and lives with her husband and one child in the same village.

Since I grew up in the town, I've not had to face any of these difficulties. I haven't even had the pressure of marriage. Yes, of course there was some prejudice, but nothing like the kind my family have to face every day in the village. For example, I did have problems with getting my scholarship as they didn't believe I was a Dalit, because my grandfather had a good job and some money. But once that was sorted out, things have been fine. I managed to graduate with a degree in science, microbiology and botany. I haven't been able to continue with my education because my grandparents can't afford to support me and my brother any more, so I haven't realised my dream of being a teacher. It would cost a lot of money to continue my education, and my parents see no sense in educating me because I should be married. So I have recently begun looking for work. I tried to get a job with the police department, but I failed the entry exam by three marks, and I have no money to pay them to take me on. I know that some of the high caste Hindus failed by more than 50 per cent but because their parents have money they've been able to bribe the police force to train them.

Once I get a job, I hope to take my parents away from the village because they suffer owing to poverty and superstition. Since I have grown up in the town, I can see how badly my people are treated by the Brahmins. Whenever I visit my parents' village I feel angry and often get into conflict with them. It hurts my heart to see my mother doing dirty work, removing dead animals and bodies. I ask her to refuse to do this work, but she just looks at me, and says: "How else can I earn money?" It's hard to accept that my people continue to do this work. I want to be able to tell them to stop being Hindu, leave the village and convert to Buddhism, but they don't understand.

In and Out of the Slums

Toughened to the bone
Survived the railway slums
Slum success story

My grandparents were the first generation of my family to convert to Buddhism, so my father was born a Buddhist, and my brothers and sisters and I were born Buddhist too. However, my parents knew nothing about Buddhism; we were just Buddhist in name. We had a picture of Babasaheb and my parents had faith in him, but as a child I never knew why. They still embraced all the Hindu gods and superstitions. My father didn't have a good job. He worked as a cleaner in a factory and earned a few rupees. My mother stayed at home and looked after all the children, cooking and cleaning.

I was born 30 years ago in the slums of a major city in Maharashtra. The slums were beside the railways and were full of huts made of straw and dung, and small houses made of corrugated iron. They were in rows and when you stepped out of your home you were almost in someone else's home. There was no drainage and no fresh water, and there were only four public toilets for a community of three thousand families or more. That meant that many people went to the toilet in the streets and on the edge of the slums. There was no school for us in the slum, and if parents encouraged their children to attend school they had to travel over an hour to the next district for their education.

Most of the people in my slum were uneducated and had minimal culture. People spoke to each other disgustingly. There was no respect for each other. Slum dwellers called each other bastards, and even harsher language was used in front of us children. The adults were rough with each other, which had a major influence on the young people. People didn't think or care about each other, they just cared for themselves. Every day I left my home to go to school or run an errand there would be a quarrel in the alley.

The state corporation gave very little attention to those of us who lived in the slums. They only gave us one water tap for all the families to share. This was often the situation in all the slums in the big cities of Maharashtra. The corporation monitored this tap with great stinginess. They turned it on early in the morning, around 4 a.m. and switched the water off at 8 a.m. The tap wasn't accessible; most families had to walk at least half an hour to get to it. My parents were quiet people and avoided conflict. But whenever I went to help with the water there was always a fight. There were always some people in the queue who didn't get any water, because when 8 a.m. came that was it, not a drip more from the tap. I begged my family to go earlier, so we began waking at 4 a.m. to ensure we would get fresh water and miss the conflict. Since the corporation did nothing about the drainage situation, I would often wake up to neighbours shouting, because dirty water from one house would run under the door of another.

Most Dalit people of my age who grew up in the cities are from the slums. Today, we still have many slums and the situation is still very much the same. Children were always fighting, especially the boys. They formed gangs and would beat each other up, drink alcohol and abuse the young women in the slums. Although the girls didn't hang around in gangs like the boys, we did still fight among ourselves. Often I would come home crying to my parents because somebody had given me a good beating. But they were angry with me for doing this.

They would shout : "You fight them, and don't come home and tell us about your troubles. Fight your own battles and learn to face your own difficulties." You had to be tough to survive in the slums, because your parents couldn't protect you.

People were always stealing from each other, including the children. This was the culture, people always stealing from their friends and family. People had no dignity or self-respect. Often I had my books and shoes stolen. When I came home crying to my parents they would beat me and say: "You take care of your things. Who told you to give them away?" So I had to learn ways of not losing my things. Sometimes I would go to school barefoot to make sure my shoes weren't stolen. Even your best friends stole from you.

My school life began when I was seven. I attended a school paid for by the state. That meant that us Dalits from the slums had to pay very little. We were in class with Brahmins and other high caste Hindus. My first day at school was fantastic and my second day too, but after that I got picked on, along with the other Dalit children. On the third day, some of my friends' parents came to the school to pick their children up and asked me what my name was. As soon as I mentioned my name, they withdrew and said: "You're an 'Untouchable'." The next day my friends behaved strangely towards me and chanted "You're a Dalit, a *Mahar*, an 'Untouchable'." But we still played together. We were too young to understand what it all meant.

However, when I was ten, some high caste girls were more spiteful. They refused to sit with me, eat with me or even play with me. And by the time I was 13, things became more obvious. It was clear who the Dalits were, as most of us were poor and from the slums. I had only one school uniform which my mother washed every evening for the next day. I wore this same shirt for a year, and it became grey, and began to fray and tear. My mother patched it with an old shirt that I had grown out of. I was so shy about this that I tried to hide the patches with my long hair, which I wore in two braids. But the higher caste girls teased me about my grey shirt and discovered my trick. They would come up behind me and pull my braids off my shoulders and show my poverty to the whole class. Everyone would laugh at my patches. I felt inferior among the high caste Hindus and had very little confidence at school. I sometimes refused to go, but my parents made me. My whole family was discriminated against at school; my younger brother and older sister got teased along with all the other Dalits.

When I became a teenager, my life began to change. My body began to mature and men began looking at me differently. Most of the homes in the slums were open plan, which meant anybody could look in and see you bathing. The bathroom in my home just had a sarong cloth to surround it, and no roof, and it was at the back of the house, exposed to all the neighbours. My next door neighbour had a beautiful wife and some beautiful children too. But every day when I took a bath he would come and watch me. He was able to enter the bathroom unnoticed by my parents, because it was easy to enter the houses in the slums. I began having bad dreams. I often dreamed that I was going to murder him. I would be standing over him with a sharp shining knife in my hand. I told my mother and father, but they didn't say anything. He came most days, and I was helpless. A similar thing used to happen in the public toilets. Men and older boys would climb up the side and watch the young ladies go to the toilet. After the third or fourth time this happened, I was so angry that I took the tin pot we used for flushing and threw it at the man's head. I ran home distraught, and when my parents asked what was wrong, I told them. But my father said: "I can't do anything. We don't have the money to build a toilet in our home, or an enclosed bathroom."

I began to feel nervous and was really angry with my parents, because I wanted them to go out and quarrel with the men who were harassing me. But they never did. They were passive and did very little. They were unable to make things better for me. This made me realise I had to look after myself, nobody was going to help with this predicament. So I worked out when the neighbour was out at work and took my bath then, and I would wait for dark till I went to the toilet. I didn't care that my stomach hurt; I wasn't going to defecate outside. So I just held on till the evening and then went. My body got used to it.

I did have the courage to tell some of my friends, and this was a revelation, because I realised that the same thing was happening to many of them too, and this made some of my friendships stronger. In fact, friendships were very important in the slums. I still have many of these friends in my life now. When you grow up as I did, it's important to have people who know where you come from, understand your childhood life, and the struggles and pain you had to go through. Many of us were in the slums till our mid 20s.

All the families were superstitious; it was part of the village culture that my parents' generation brought to the slums. Nobody made much use of the medical room in the slum; people relied on traditional practices. This made life frightening, to the extent that my brother almost died. He was a year younger than me, and he became sick when he was twelve. My father sent for a man to heal him. This man looked at my brother, and then asked my father to bring a bowl of water. He blew on the water for five minutes, and then told my brother to drink it. We all watched eagerly for positive results. But the next day my brother was in more pain. My father told him to be patient, but I could see he was very sick. Without our parents' consent we went in secret to the clinic in the slum. The doctor checked him over and then said to me: "Your brother is very sick. He has to be admitted into the hospital immediately, otherwise he may die." An hour after he was admitted his appendix burst. He was in hospital for two months because my father had wasted time believing in Hindu practices.

Everyone in the slum regularly worshipped many gods, and I too took up the practice of worship from an early age. I used to go every day with one of my parents to watch people give money and food to Ganesh. Even when I was old enough to go without my parents, I still went with my brothers and sisters. We continued to worship the gods because we could eat the food people offered, and it was much better than what we ate at home.

In the end I was fortunate to change my Hindu conditioning because of education. I managed to get my caste certificate which had 'Ex-Mahar – Untouchable' on it so I could get a scholarship for further education. I was one of the few girls who studied beyond 16 in my slum. But first I had to avoid marriage. My elder sister was married, and there was pressure from my father about me. But my older brother was able to convince my father that I was clever and he should let me continue my studies. I chose to do social work, and graduated with an MA. I began attending lectures about Dr. Ambedkar and after two or three months, I realised I wanted to do something for my community and for my society. I was 22 and till then had only thought about earning money, buying a good house and having a family, but these lectures inspired me. I knew I couldn't be like some Dalit people who do well in education, get a good job and forget about where they've come from, forget about the suffering of their people. That's like the slum mentality all over again – just think about yourself and nobody else. I felt I had a duty to help my community, a duty to continue Babasaheb's work and not forget what he did.

I returned to the slums and began working with the people. Although my slum was developed eight years ago, and the conditions are much better for people growing up there now, there are still many slums, and many of the parents who live there don't value education at all. The women in the slums have very little confidence, and part of my work has been to tell them: "Don't look at me and think I've always looked like this in my sari made of good cloth. I came from the slums and have had my difficulties. You can become like me. I had to do it alone. My father died by the time I was 15, and so my brother left education to support us all." I try to encourage them to take advantage of the scholarships and not to believe that because they are poor they can't change their lives. I come from a poor family in the slums, so I am able to understand their lives. This is why I want to help my community.

I am now happily married with one child, though both my parents have died. I work for the Arya Tara Mahila Trust (ATMT), a women's organisation based in Pune but serving women in many states. We work with women and children from the slums. We are helping these families to develop small-scale businesses, following the principle of 'trade not aid'. And we have a project to tackle the huge problem of domestic violence in India.

We are also actively engaged in teaching and promoting Buddhism and the teachings of the Buddha. We also teach women computer studies, so that they have an opportunity to become independent. We realise that because of the Dalit woman's poverty and her caste conditioning, she feels inferior and finds it hard to face personal difficulties. The caste system disempowers our women, to the extent that they find it hard to take the initiative.

Since ATMT and our sister charities like Bahujan Hitay have been founded, we have helped many women in the slums and villages to change their lives. However I realise that we Indian women must help ourselves. Babasaheb said: "Caste is a state of mind." I believe that we Dalit women throughout India have to change our minds, retrain our minds. We must realise that we are not Dalits because of bad karma. We must free our minds of superstitions and Hindu gods if we are truly to change our destinies.

Head cupped in hands
With TV, hi fi and kids
Corrugated slum

I am 17 years old and still live in the slum I was born in. We are all Dalits but most of us are Hindus, with a few Muslims, Christians and Buddhists. Look around for yourself, you can see what it looks like. Over there are the railways. Look at the houses. They're just one room, and made of this corrugated iron. By the railway, they are made of sticks and plastic. My mother, father, brother, three sisters and I all grew up in a room this big. My mother still works in domestic service for the higher caste people, and my father works as a cleaner on the railways over there. Sometimes my father drinks, and then he starts a fight with my mother, but she is able to fight back.

My parents treated me well. They encouraged me to go to school and get my education. Every day I would wake at six, go to school at seven, come home at one, have lunch, and do some domestic work like cleaning and cooking. I also helped a neighbour pack snacks to sell at their shop, and if there was time, I would play hide and seek and hopping games with my friends. I didn't mind working while going to school because my parents needed the money. It made me happy when I could come home and give them what I earned, so my mother could buy the things she needed for our home. I learned to sew when very young, so was able to make clothes and sell them

When I was eleven, I left school, and then my grandmother arranged my marriage. She prepared me very well. She told me: "There is a Hindu man who is very good. He lives in a slum on the other side of the city, and he earns money, and he will take good care of you. I know he is a good man, because he has taken responsibility for paying for his younger sister's wedding." This was pleasing to hear, as some of my friends had married bad men who had no work and couldn't look after them properly. I felt certain that my husband was going to be a good man and support me. But I was also scared and wondered how my husband's family would treat me. It was a troubled time before I married because I was apprehensive and didn't want to go and live in a strange family's house.

The first time I spoke to him, I was very nervous. It was on the day of my wedding. I did enjoy the sweets, flowers and music, but I couldn't say much, as my mother-in-law was not kind to me. I had no idea how old my husband was, but he looked as big as my eldest brother, who was 25. The first thing I said to my husband was: "Why is your mother so nasty to me?" He said: "Don't mind her. Everything will be fine." So my nerves calmed down. I went to live in her house with him, but after one week my mother-in-law began insulting me. She would scream at me and say: "You can't cook. Your grandmother has cheated us. You're a slum prostitute."

My husband told me not to worry; she would become kinder to me. We lived in one room in her house, and then we moved into a separate house with my husband's brother and sister-in-law. The slum was cleaner and things were much better, till I had my first child. Then my husband began to come home late. When I asked where he had been, he would say: "Don't worry about me" and then beat me. I became frightened. I wondered what kind of husband I had got. This must be because of my bad karma, I thought. I must have got him because I did something bad in my life. I wanted to run away to my mother's house, but I didn't know how to, and I was dependent on him for money.

There was nobody I could speak to. I had no friends nearby. When I was pregnant with my second child my husband refused to keep me. He said he couldn't pay for my keep any more, and sent me back to the slums where I grew up. My mother was understanding. She said: "Stay with me. You have two children and you must bring them up well." But I am still very sad, because all I want is to live with my husband. I don't want to be like all the other young slum girls who have failed marriages. In the first year after I moved back to my slum, he never came looking for me. I was worried about my children and how I would manage to feed them. Then one day he came to my mother's home late at night, banging on the door and screaming so everybody in the slum could hear him. He was asking for money, like many of the other young husbands in my slum. I realised then that my family had not paid any dowry and this was why he and his family were angry with me. My parents had no money for dowry, and my mother insisted that my husband's family had agreed to some arrangement, but now they wanted to change their minds. My grandmother said she gave them money, but after I had two children the family became greedy and wanted more money. My grandmother said to me: "What can I do? It's traditional to marry. I married you to someone I considered was good. But there is nothing I can do. I am sad about this because I thought he was a good man but I can't even recognise him now."

I am lucky because my family have accepted me back. Many of my friends have nowhere to go, and people in the slum look at them badly. My family are supporting me. My husband still comes to the house at night filled with drink and demands money. He shouts to my parents: "You have my wife inside there, so you give me some money." He's not taking any care of me or my children. My parents have to try and support me. I don't want to be on my own like a widow; everyone will think something is wrong with me. I want him to change. My grandmother says: "It's just fate that this happens to so many young women." She says the only way I can change things is if I go to court. But I have no money, so I live in fear that my husband may harm all my family because of the dowry.

From slums to heaven
Street hawker to activist
First ladies' union

I was the fourth daughter of my family. Because of this, I got no recognition in my family. Nobody attended to me, since I was a curse, and they wanted a son. When I married, my situation got worse. I was just used as a tool for sex. I had no education. I thought: this is my life, this must be the life that all women have to live. I was living in the largest slum in Asia. It's called Dharavi and it's in Mumbai. It's full of Hindus from the Dalit communities. Living there was like living in hell. You can't imagine what it's like living in a slum that expands every day, with huts built on top of your roof, huts in front of your door. It was a very dirty life. People defecated in front of your door, on your roof. The slum was built on a creek, and beside a cremation ground where dead bodies were burned daily. People made illegal liquor in huge containers, and fought for water every day. The state government charged us a rupee for one pot of water a day, and there were no lights, and only the water from the creek to bathe and wash your clothes in.

I moved from that slum in 1993. I needed to get out of that hell. I knew if I didn't, I would die there. I had taught myself to read and discovered that another world existed in Mumbai. My husband enjoyed his life, staying out late at night or not coming home at all. I managed to find where he socialised and insisted that if he spent all his time in a better part of the city, there was no reason why his family couldn't join him. He worked in the central public department of Maharashtra and mixed with a different crowd in the posh area of Mumbai, Malabar Hill.

His friend managed to find a room for us and our children. The first day we moved there I couldn't believe it. I woke up and it felt like heaven. I had never before opened my eyes and seen skyscrapers and trees, and it was so clean. I was in paradise. I got up, looked out of the window and could see nothing but beauty. I had never walked onto a balcony and looked up at the blue sky, and that first morning I did all of that. There was even a big sea in front of me, and women walked below my balcony in clean and beautiful clothes, wearing nice jewellery.

I couldn't believe I had survived almost twenty years breathing in sewage, stepping over human excrement every day of my life. I felt moved to write, and found myself writing poems in my head. I even wrote some lines down: "I felt a world of gold, swans eating the pearls, but the poor crows die of hunger." All this was going on in my mind, new thoughts I had never heard in my head before. But my husband was not interested in me and my thoughts, and my children were too young to understand.

I was lonely in this new home. At least in the slums people communicated with you. I was the poor Dalit lady of the block of flats I lived in and nobody wanted to speak to me. I was a prisoner in my one room. I longed for company. I would walk onto the balcony and begin speaking to the trees and the flowers, and they became my teachers. I had never noticed nature before, and I was affected by all the seasonal changes.

I wrote poems for myself, and one day was introduced to a famous writer who looked at them and encouraged me to write. She told me I wrote so well and had such wonderful qualities. These words were like an oasis in a desert – they changed my life forever. Nobody had ever encouraged me or spoken well of me before. She told me I should write my autobiography, but how could I? I had no rich experience to share. I wasn't famous. I was just a housewife from the slums. Who would be interested in my book? I had no name in the literary world. How could I earn a living from writing?

When I thought about all this, I realised there was one thing I could do – something quite different from writing. I could make *bhakari* (bread made by village people) and people would buy and eat them. One day, when I had extra food left over from the family meal, I had the confidence to pack a tiffin box (lunch box) and go to the Assembly Rooms where people gathered at lunch time. I saw some large stones and placed a piece of wood on top, and opened up my tiffin. I couldn't believe it. The taxi drivers stopped to buy my food. I made Rs. 70 ($150) on that first day. The next day I cooked rice and dal, and the taxi drivers stopped again and bought my food. They told me how good it was to eat home cooking made with clean oil. It was a success, and I realised I had found something that I was good at and I could earn money from. I had finally liberated myself from the slum mentality. I was no longer dependent on my husband, and it didn't matter if he drank all his wages. I could now feed my children properly.

I set up a proper table on the street, and began to attract many regulars, but I was harassed by the male hawkers on the streets. They were jealous of me being a lady, and didn't think I had the right to be there. It was another new world, a world of police and municipal agents. I couldn't understand why I had to give money to the agents or the police so I could work. A male friend suggested I join the general union for hawkers but I soon realised that women needed a union for themselves. So in 2003 I set up the first Hawkers' Union for Ladies. I knew there must be other ladies like me who were being cheated by the police and exploited by the system. And I couldn't fight on my own. Ladies were often picked on. If a lady hawker had an unauthorised stall, the municipal corporation would pick it up and dump it in a hall. If this ever happened to the men, they could go the same day and pay a small fine and get their goods back. With us ladies it was different. We would be told that the clerk was not available, or told to wait for a few hours, but nobody would turn up, or we'd be asked to come back the next day. Men could bribe but ladies had to beg. Dalit ladies have often tried to sell things on the streets, like vegetables, fruits, bangles and clothes. But we have been treated badly, money has been stolen from us, and we are harassed by male hawkers.

In the history of India, hawkers have always been from lower caste backgrounds. We are all from the Scheduled Castes, Other Backward Castes and Tribal Castes. We are all from a poor background and traditionally this has been the only independent work we can do. My union has been extremely active in the few years that it has existed. I have 250 members and all of them are protected. My union is arguing for reservations for lady hawkers. The citizens of Mumbai went to the High Court and said that hawkers should not be allowed to sell on the streets. So the High Court conducted a survey of the situation in Mumbai. When I heard about this, I wrote a letter on International Women's Day, which is dedicated to the hard-working women of the world, and suggested to the commission that they give women 50 per cent reservations. They acknowledged my request and suggested in their survey that we should be given 30 per cent reservations. This has recently been submitted to the High Court.

I've also sent a letter off to the Railway Minister of India, suggesting that there should be at least one stall given to women on every station in India. I have been invited to Delhi to discuss this with the minister.

I believe in proper reservations for women, and my union is in a debate with the state government about a new shopping mall they want to build in Mumbai, where the old cotton mills were demolished. We are asking that there should be one floor for the women of the mill workers' families. Mumbai's wealth came from the cotton mills, and these women gave so much from their own hands, but many of them are now forced to work on the streets selling as nobody will employ them. The state government gave them no pensions, not a single penny, when the mills were closed down.

My dream is for the Dalit lady to become completely independent. This will be such an achievement for women like me who came from the slums and were totally dependent on their husbands' income, or worked for other people doing domestic work. If I had stayed in the slums, I would not be doing the work I do now.

If the High Court agrees to give 30 per cent reservations to lady hawkers on the streets, and a one metre zone for each of us, I will be very happy. It will be like leaving the slums again. Reservations for women hawkers have never been asked for in the history of India. If we can own one metre of land, this will change our lives radically. It will live on after today's ladies die, and our daughters and granddaughters will reap the benefit of being completely independent of their husbands or the high caste employers. If we ladies become independent, we may even earn enough to move out of the slums.

Arts and Culture

She's from the oppressed
Experience is threefold
A Dalit writer

I was born in a village in the Konkan, a place in Maharashtra which is famous for mangoes. My father was educated till the age of 18 and became a teacher, and then he married my mother. She was illiterate, but she knew how to weave baskets to earn money for our family. I'm the youngest of six children: three girls and three boys. My father told my mother to educate all of us, and not to let us sit at home. One of my brothers died when I was eight, and my father died when I was nine, so we were left with hardly any money. We could scarcely afford to eat, as we were dependent on his small income. So my mother went out to work and fulfilled her husband's wish by educating all of us from the money she earned from the baskets.

My mother was very careful with money. True, we were poor, but she would choose not to give us good food or good clothes, or send us on trips with the school. She was always thinking: "I must save money so I don't have to ask people to give it to me." So she wouldn't spend money on us unnecessarily. But all the village people were poor. They used to cut hay, wood and grass, and bring it to the city to sell, and then they bought the things they needed for their families. I would listen to adults at the market talking and I would keep all these things in my mind, but I had no idea I would write stories later in my life. I had no idea I could write.

Many years later, I married and had children. My husband worked in a post office. I still didn't think of writing, or sharing my feelings or those of other people. But then I read Dr. Ambedkar's biography and his book, *The Buddha and His Dhamma*. Before I read these books, I couldn't understand why my people were oppressed by casteism. I didn't understand the 'Untouchability' I experienced as a child. When my mother gave me her baskets to sell, I knocked at the Brahmins' doors. They didn't allow me to go inside. They said: "Stay here." They would throw money into my hand, so as not to touch me, and they would pour water on the baskets too, and on the floor, before accepting them. I was angry, and sometimes asked: "Why won't you touch me?" But they never replied. Discrimination existed, but I didn't understand why. But Dr. Ambedkar's biography gave me the answer. The hierarchy, the discrimination, is because of caste, because of the four-varna system. Then I realised I must share my thoughts and my 'Untouchable' experience, and share the situation of women struggling with casteism and patriarchy.

From 1975 I began to write stories. I was 31 years old. During this time I was working in the state government office for women. I worked with a woman who had five daughters and no sons. She wasn't allowed a family planning operation till she had a boy; she had to have a son if she wanted a hysterectomy. So I discussed this subject in my writing. My first book was called *Sixth Finger*, a collection of short stories exploring some of these issues. I wrote stories about women in general, dealing with dowry, domestic violence and the curse of girl children. But because I hadn't focused on casteism, other writers said I wasn't a Dalit writer, but just a writer, and therefore I was boycotted and not invited to speak at any Dalit programmes. Of course, caste issues are part of my life, but I also have experience as a Dalit woman who is oppressed by everyone in her society.

One day I was asked to tell a story at a Dalit conference, so I modified a story I had written to include the theme of Dr. Ambedkar's movement. It was about a servant and his owner. The owner had written a play, and one of his actors had died. He told his servant to come and take his role, the role of the Hindu god Rama. Because the owner had treated him badly, the servant refused to do it. He said: "I have dignity. I could play this role, but I will not, because you have given me a lot of trouble. I will not play Rama's role because Rama is not our god. When Ambedkar and my people tried to enter the temples you wouldn't let us in, and the gods have never supported our people." People liked this story very much, and there were big cheers from the audience. So finally I got the name of a Dalit writer. This was important to me as I am from the Dalit community and have experienced great oppression in my life because of this.

A Dalit writer is someone who has experience of casteism and discrimination. Caste is nothing, caste is only imagination, but people still believe in it. As Dalit writers, we are challenging this imagination, because we want dignity and humanity. When someone writes about casteism from their own experience, this means they are a Dalit writer. Brahmins have taken the subject of casteism, but they are not Dalit writers because it is not their own experience. If I write about black people's experience, I'm not a black writer because these experiences are not my own. The individual must go through the experience.

I've had a lot of experience of casteism. You can look at me now and think: "She's living in this nice apartment, she has decent clothes, she has some money," but people still don't respect me. So we are struggling for this. My daughter is struggling for her dignity. She is capable, but denied because she is a Dalit, and her children are suffering too.

I have a short story collection called *Fourth Wall* which looks at how people can't mix with each other because of the walls of caste. Dr. Ambedkar said: "Casteism is like a building with four floors and no staircase, because people can't go from one floor to another. If you are born on a particular floor you die there." I took this as a theme for my collection of short stories.

I also published a short story called 'Carried Over'. This is a story about how women are taken for granted, how nobody asks them what they want to do. In this story, a woman marries her cousin, and when her husband needs a kidney, none of the relatives offer one. They just point a finger at the wife, because as the wife, it's her duty and she should give it to him. Her two sons are there but they will not offer to give a kidney to their father. They all run away, leaving the wife no choice. She has to give up her job and independence to help her husband. When the husband goes into hospital he writes a will and asks her to sign it. The will says that everything will go to her two sons, and the sons should look after her. But the woman knows that this will not happen. Her sons would not give her one farthing. She realises before the transplant that she is also at risk of not surviving. She says to herself, "We are both at death's door and he is not thinking of me. Why should my sons have the property? This is my property also." So she burns the paper.

One of my stories has caused a stir. I have written about the women from my village who sell mangoes and how men come up and say: "Show me your mangoes. How big are they? How small are they? How good or bad are they? Are they sweet or salty?" One of the lady's sons, who is 12, asks: "Why do men behave like this?" This story was accepted on a BA syllabus. But there was an outcry from a women's organisation founded by the Brahmins. They protested and said: "It's an unsuitable story for a women's college. How can this be on the syllabus?" But the student federation objected because they said it was about their experience, and it would not have a bad effect on their minds. There were many articles about this, and the students said: "We understand this experience. What rubbish are you talking?"

My brother has five daughters, and my mother says he must have a son. I wrote a story about this situation. It was about a woman who was fed up after having five daughters. When she was pregnant for the sixth time, she prayed for a boy. When she was admitted to hospital to give birth she thought to herself: "How can I change my child? – because I know I'm going to have a girl." This thought was hammering in her head. It happened that there was a young girl next to her who was about to give birth. She called to the nurse and said: "Don't call the doctor when I'm ready to give birth; let me do it on my own. If I have a girl and the young girl next door has a boy, you have to swap them. You just keep quiet about it." The nurse tried to convince her that she would have a boy but the lady said: "This is my sixth child. I know the symptoms by now. It's going to be a girl." She offered the nurse jewellery and money, and the nurse gave in. When she gave birth, it was a girl, and the young girl gave birth to a boy, and so the nurse swapped them. When her family came they celebrated and were so pleased she had had a baby boy. They said: "Oh, we knew definitely that you would have a son; we prayed to so many gods for this; this is the fruit of our prayers."

That night, after they left her in hospital, she was woken up by a cry. It was the baby girl crying next door. She got up and told the young mother to look after her daughter, but the girl just fell back to sleep. Again the child cried, and she wondered why the mother wasn't taking care of her baby, so she asked the nurse. The nurse said: "Don't you know why she's not caring for this child? She is not married. Nobody knows who the father is. Somebody has deceived her, and now they say they will murder the baby." The woman was shocked. What to do? She told the girl: "You take care of this child. If you made a mistake, don't make another mistake now. Don't abandon her." The girl's mother overheard and said: "You look after your own son." But she kept trying to save the child. She told the girl to have her child adopted if she couldn't look after her. When she left the hospital she was anxious, not knowing what her real daughter's fate would be. At the same time her family were all joyful. The story ends with this question, the pain of both mothers.

I really connected to Dr. Ambedkar's movement during the mid-1980s, while I was studying for my Masters in Marathi literature. After I graduated, I thought I would like a doctorate. This was a craze at that time – every educated Dalit wanted a PhD because Dr. Ambedkar had said: "Men and women must be educated, we must educate ourselves, take something from society and get our dignity. Then we will be something, otherwise we will remain in the same position." While thinking about his movement, I thought: "All those years ago, men were obviously part of Ambedkar's movement, but what about the women? Surely women must also have been involved." I began to research this question, but I couldn't see much in Ambedkar's biography about the women – only the odd page here and there – so I decided I would research my doctorate on the subject of women in the Ambedkarite movement. I put a paper together and presented it to my professor, but he said: "You can't take this subject, because your MA is in literature. You will have to do an MA in social sciences; then you can do it."

I told one of my friends from the women's liberation movement about this, and she said: "Why take a doctorate? Write a book. This is important. Take a friend with you to do interviews with the women, and I'll help you find out where these women are today." I met with some opposition from the men in the movement. They said: "Why are you searching here and there for women? Are you going mad? There were no women in the movement. It was a men's movement. Don't waste your energy and time." But I didn't let this put me off. I wrote an article in a magazine for International Women's Day, 8th March, to get interest. Mostly the women were in Maharashtra, but some of them had moved to Delhi, Chennai and Kolapur, so I had to travel the whole of India. I travelled with a friend of mine, who was a housewife, to do this work. For three years I conducted my research and I met these ladies and interviewed them about their work in the movement. There were often tears in their eyes when I met them, and there was a lot of crying. "You came to us, you recognise us, and you're interested in our work? Our husbands were beating us and telling us not to attend meetings, not to go on marches, but we still attended and worked hard, and nobody has given us recognition." *We Made History Too* came out in 1989, and it's the first and only book to focus on the women who were active in Ambekar's movement when he was alive and for the next ten or fifteen years after his death.

In 2004 I published my autobiography, called *Aayadan*, which means 'weaving basket'. It's my eighth book, and it's now in its 5th edition. It took me thirty years to write it because I used to think that there wasn't enough to say about my life to fill a whole book. So I just wrote short stories. I also wrote small publications about Dr. Ambedkar and about Buddhism. When I came to Mumbai in the 70s, there was so much happening in the city and so many stories were being written that I thought: "Why would my story be important?" The women's liberation movement was very active, and many of these women were doing programmes and conventions, so I felt intimidated. The stories they told made me realise the level of discrimination between men and women, which is different from casteism. I began to understand male domination clearly, and learned more about burned dowry cases and women who had been stabbed or had committed suicide. Members of the Women's Liberation movement were campaigning and writing articles about all these things.

When I listened very well and carefully I began to understand women's liberation, and so I began to write about these things too. I realised I had a lot to say about casteism, male domination, office surroundings, patriarchy and reservations. I had many things to say which were humiliating to me as a woman. And then I looked at the women who still lived in the villages, struggling with poverty, so I collected all these experiences. But I felt I couldn't write about these things explicitly then because I had to focus on being a Dalit writer. It was when I began writing my childhood experience in a children's magazine and the editors asked why I wasn't writing my autobiography that I began to think about all the information I had collected over the past 28 years. I realised I had enough to fill a book. I also wrote about quarrels with my husband, how he dominated me, how my children treated me. The book has become a bestseller in India.

Now I'm going to write my first novel, exploring the theme of the female activist, the experiences she has in her family life, her thoughts about the movement, and how she is influenced by Dr. Ambedkar. I have experience of Dalit people who think that Ambedkar said that you take part in politics just to get some rights and have a good life. This is the message people are taking, and that's the basis of a lot of political parties. Their motto is 'Fighting against caste', and they say caste must vanish, but these same people are against inter-caste marriage. So the protagonist in my novel will ask: "Why are these people so focused on politics as the way out of casteism?"

Writing is my life. I think about the protagonist of my novel every day. I am proud to be a Dalit writer, and will do my bit in the movement to educate people about the tragedies of caste. I hope my literature will help people to understand why we are oppressed, and how we can come out of this oppression. I hope Dalit women will understand their threefold oppression of caste, patriarchy and poverty, and how they can begin to free themselves from male domination. I hope that Dalit writers will be part of the movement to help caste vanish from the whole of India.

> *She's educated*
> *Professor in her own right*
> *But still oppressed*

I'm a professor of Dalit literature and the head of Marathi at Nagpur University. I was also born a Dalit, and grew up immersed in Buddhist culture. I became involved with literature through working in the women's movement and had the opportunity to visit tribal areas and help with the situation of women. While visiting the tribal area of Corku, I came across a tribe called Bolai, and discovered that it was part of the Dalit community. I was soon made aware that this tribe was unknown to the Maharashtra region, and felt intrigued to research this culture through the folklore. It seemed the best way to try and understand their culture. I was especially fascinated to find out something about the Dalit woman's lineage. It is extremely difficult to write about Dalit women's literature which existed before the 1950s because very little of it was written down. So I decided to do my doctorate in folk literature in the hope that this would add to the body of Dalit literature which has become quite prevalent in the past 50 years.

I gathered much of my material by going to the villages and talking to the women. They performed poetry, sang and passed stories down to their children. They performed at marriages, births and traditional festivals, and sang to their babies to send them to sleep. One of the rhymes I recorded was the following.

> *Do not go to the Brahmins' place*
> *They have holy books to read*
> *And rich food to eat*
> *And we don't have the time.*

I heard this performed at a wedding ceremony. In it, a woman is advising her son that if he goes to the Brahmins' marriage ceremony he will be discriminated against and endure prejudice. This is her warning. Much of the literature is from the women's point of view, and focuses on the cycle of life in Hindu culture.

When the Dalit woman in the village performs or writes, her art is different from that of the Dalit woman from the cities, because her circumstances are different. The Dalit women of this tribe were immersed in Hindu culture and had never heard of Dr. Ambedkar or Buddhism. The concerns of the Dalit woman living in the villages today are not that dissimilar, depending on how she perceives herself. She may be fortunate enough to have a water supply, a toilet and electricity, but this is all. She still lives in the corner of the village where she has access to only the basic provisions.

There are several types of attitude in the village. There is the Dalit woman who knows why she is poor and is aware of Dr. Ambedkar. There is the Dalit woman who thinks she is Hindu and is poor because of her karma. And there is the Dalit woman who knows she is a Dalit and thinks she is poor because of Brahministic scriptures that have made her an outcaste. These different women perform, sing and pass down stories according to their different attitudes and points of view.

They also write about abuse. I have also worked on the

government committee and part of my role is working with victims of rape. I am often called upon to be a mediator for Dalit women, and help to support them by taking them to the police station and making sure their complaints are recorded. I have some influence because although the police may know I'm a Dalit, I have the power which comes from writing for a newspaper about the situation of Dalit women, and the police don't want to be exposed.

Sixty to seventy per cent of Dalit women are raped in the village community, mainly by higher caste people. The Dalit woman is perceived to be stupid by the higher caste people. She is more vulnerable than a high caste woman because her life isn't secure; she often works alone in the fields and is from a poor background. High caste women are protected. They have good support networks, money and confidence. If such abuse happens to them they have the confidence and money to do something about it. The Dalit woman in the village knows that the police will treat her unfairly, and that they will rarely take any action against Brahmins or other high caste Hindus. I often meet the women, take them to the station and insist that the police make a file and arrest the man. The police know who I am, and know that I also work on the women's committee and that I can go above their heads. So it's in their interest to record the crime and not lose the file.

When a woman tries to find work, she is only given cleaning and washing. Brahmin families may employ her to do domestic work, but they will not employ a Dalit to cook for them. They still believe she is polluted. Some Brahmins still go as far as not letting a Dalit woman touch their utensils, and will purify the house after she has done her work and left for the day. Dalit women in the cities are still facing discrimination too. For example, if a woman opts for a job in an office, the bosses, who are normally of higher caste, will try to suppress her, and will do anything to prevent her from being promoted. If a Dalit woman is educated like me, she can still suffer discrimination. We're often told we have our position because of government reservations. People make it their business to tell us we didn't get our job because of our intelligence, and that we have poor living standards so we won't know how to behave in the job, or maintain the standard needed to do it. In my own case, I have often been told that I am only able to be a professor because of government reservation places. "You're from the Scheduled Caste, that's why you passed." The fact is that everyone who is a professor has to take the National Eligibility test, and if you pass this you can become a professor. I didn't have to show my Scheduled Caste certificate to become a professor. I had to work very hard like everybody else who has this title.

I still suffer because of my caste, even though I am highly educated. It was difficult for me to rent a house; as soon as people realised my caste I was asked to leave. When I managed to find an apartment for my family to live in, I was surrounded by high caste Hindus. One day I wanted to visit the village, and I left my pot with neighbours and asked them to collect my milk for the next day. When my daughter went to pick up the milk the next day, they threw the pot down at her feet, spilling all the milk. Even now that I own my house, I still suffer discrimination. I needed a cleaner because I have two children and both my husband and I go out to work. When I approached several cleaners from my own Dalit community, their Brahmin employers told them that if they came to work for me, they would terminate their employment.

Inter-caste marriage is still frowned upon. I married out of my caste; my husband is from a higher caste than me. When I met his parents, his mother said: "My son may accept you as a wife, but I will never accept you as a daughter-in-law. I will never allow you to touch my kitchen." It was a love marriage. I met my husband because he was working for the Dalit movement. He was a journalist and writer and connected to the Dalit theatre so I was confident about our relationship. All his friends were Dalit people, and we were in the same social circles. It seemed natural to fall in love with him. My in-laws have softened over time, especially since my two children have been born. They even greet me with "Jai Bhim!"; it's a huge thing for them to give me a Buddhist greeting. But we are still not accepted in certain circles. We're not invited to dinners or festivals with high caste people, and my children are considered Dalit.

I have become successful through great struggle and continued determination. Every Dalit woman has to do this if she wants to succeed. A Dalit woman's talent is only recognised by her community, others will say her success is because of her caste. Brahmin women are given talent through birth. So I decided quite early that if a Brahmin woman knew one thing, I would make sure I knew ten things. I had a very good childhood. My father was an only son, so his parents were able to educate him and pay for him to attend an English school, which was rare. He became a deputy collector in the 60s. This is an officer who has responsibility for fifteen or more villages. His job was to collect the revenue and look after the development of the facilities. My mother was a housewife, but encouraged my education too. She said that all her children had to be educated as Dr. Ambedkar was. I have a brother and sister and all of us have done well professionally. My brother is a computer software engineer in Chicago, and my sister, who married a Brahmin, has a diploma in German and is an assistant manager of a company.

I am part of the first generation of Dalit women to be successful and I am extremely grateful for that. My life as an educated Dalit woman is very different from that of an educated high caste Hindu woman because she doesn't have the responsibility of the whole society. Educated Dalit women often have to ask themselves what is their social commitment to the community. We always think of our society and what we must share with it. For most of us it is important to do what we can for the uplift of our community. We feel a duty to give back and help the lakhs (hundreds of thousands) of Dalit people who are still struggling and suffering in Indian society.

I am divorced
Once was humiliated
Found voice with the pen

I became a journalist so I could fight against my relatives and the people around me. I wanted to fight against the Hindu culture which continues to oppress my people, especially the women. I wanted power and independence and discovered this through the written word.

I am a traditional girl. I come from a nomadic tribal caste who settled in a village only four decades ago. We were brought into the lowest caste of Hinduism when we settled. I was born in 1970, and growing up was a big headache for me. Ladies were never allowed out, and my people believed in all the Hindu gods. In my village this is still the situation today. Women are not encouraged to be educated, and we cannot choose our marriage. In my village, dowry is a huge problem. Sometimes the in-laws harass the families of their daughters-in-law for money, and if they are not successful, sometimes they burn their daughter-in-law. She can only escape her life when she dies in her husband's home; this is the tradition.

I had a problem when it came to my turn to be found a husband because I am very tall and men did not like this. Nobody wanted to accept me. My uncle got so angry that he threatened to chop my legs off. But eventually they found a man for me. His family demanded Rs 50,000 ($1250), and wanted a big show for the wedding. Problems began on my wedding day. The groom demanded from my father an extra Rs 500 ($12.5), a gold chain and a motor cycle, but he refused. My husband began harassing me on that day. Since my father would not give him any money he ignored me and insulted me. He left me in his parents' house and went to live in Pune. I could only visit his home with his parents. I was innocent and obeyed every rule they gave me. Whenever my husband visited I could never eat or sleep until the men had eaten and gone to bed. My cooking and cleaning were never good enough. My husband never loved me. Eventually I moved with his parents to Pune and began living with him and his family. I fell pregnant, but after three months he beat me up so much that I miscarried. He was angry because I put too much turmeric in the food. He wouldn't even take me to the hospital. He said: "It's not my problem."

My family didn't believe in divorce but my brother, who is a judge, did speak to him, and this frightened him for a while. But a few months later things at home got worse. My husband stopped speaking to me; he wouldn't even mention my name. I began to lose my emotional balance. I began to talk to myself, and say: "I don't want to live, just give me money for poison." My mother-in-law overheard me, and she said: "Here you are. Take these rupees to buy your poison." She had never given me money before. I was surprised, but I took the money and bought poison. I came home and sat in the one room while my mother-in-law sat in the kitchen. I took the poison and slashed my veins too, because I believed I had done something wrong, which was why my marriage was failing. I wrote with my own blood: "Don't punish my husband or in-laws, the gods will punish them if I'm innocent." My mother-in-law watched me do all of this, and didn't try to stop me. It wasn't until a relative of the family visited and saw all the blood that I was taken to the hospital.

I remained unconscious for three months, and I was ill for almost a year. During this time my husband said he wanted a divorce. I didn't want a divorce because I believed it meant I had no future, but it went ahead. My father-in-law gave my family back the Rs. 50,000 because they had broken the marriage. My husband was still angry, and appeared on a reality TV show which looked at women and divorce. He publicly mentioned my name and said I had ruined his life because of the divorce. This programme was seen by many people in my community, and he knew this would be a big problem for me. But I also saw the power of the media and realised that if I wanted to fight my people, I had to do something where no one could fight me. And so I became curious about the media.

Once I recovered, my parents tried to marry me off again. They introduced me to a homosexual man, to a 60-year-old, and to an alcoholic. My sister was very supportive of me during this time, and gave me the courage to refuse. I had to begin earning some money, so I attended a media conference I had heard about. At the end of the day participants were invited to conduct a spontaneous interview with someone and then submit it with a view to publication. I interviewed a man who made musical noises with a bus ticket. The organisers loved the interview so much that they called me back and invited me to a course on journalism. This was the beginning of my freedom. It was the beginning of my fight against arranged marriages, the dowry, and the situation of the Dalits in this country.

I was inspired by a Marathi journalist who bought a printing press at the age of 60. He didn't know anything about journalism, but told his friends, who mocked him, "I will learn to run the press." He set up a newspaper to fight Gandhi. I thought that if he could do this at 60, why couldn't I try to be a good journalist? So I did more study, and I joined a Dalit student group and became very active writing about the slums and poverty. Once I qualified in 2001, I was selected out of thirty people to work for a revolutionary publication for the Dalit people. It gives space for people who are fighting for their basic human rights; no other papers will take an interest in such stories as most of them are Brahmin-led. Our office has been burned down very often by the Hindu party, Shiv Sena, because we have covered stories that have spoken out against Hindu traditions. I have written stories about the situation of the Dalit woman, and I learned that the problems I have had in my life, are the problems of many Dalit women in society. I have also campaigned for nomadic tribes who are only employed to work in the cremation grounds, and other low caste work. They have no constitutional rights, and do not appear on the government register. I was the first person to cover their huge gatherings and highlight their problems. The Brahmin papers snatched the story up immediately. Before then they had shown no interest. I also cover the arts, as that is important too, and have interviewed many famous people, like the Oscar nominee Bollywood film star Atul Kulkarni and the poet Vinda Karandikar.

I am fortunate to have found myself through journalism. I am an empowered young woman. I've even had the courage to marry again, and to tell my husband about the past. He has accepted me completely, and we have two beautiful children. And I intend to continue with my career. I want to show the women I write about how to be positive and have willpower. They need to know that if they have faith in their lives as valued human beings, things will move on. From somewhere I found faith after my failed marriage, and I never again want to look back or think that my life is not worth living.

Not just a seamstress
Textile designer artist
Rare for sari girl

I am fortunate that my family encouraged me to be an artist,
because it's not a job that many women do. I'm a textile artist,
and most women from the Dalit community are only familiar
with sewing. I've learnt how to make different embroideries,
using advanced printing techniques, batik and specialist
techniques from other states like Gujarat. I am not limited to
the needle and thread like most Indian women.

When I was in school I enjoyed drawing and sketching very
much, and my teachers saw that I had a natural ability, and
encouraged me to buy books about art. My father would ask
the local stationers to tell him when any new books about art or
design appeared, and my mother gave me a beautiful paint-box
when I was a child. She also encouraged me to make *rangolis*.
A *rangoli* is a traditional form of art in India, often made on
auspicious days. *Rangolis* are made on the ground outside the
front door, to welcome the gods and goddesses into the home.
Traditionally they come from the tribal people of India who
made designs on their walls and the floors inside their home.
They were made from rice paste. When the poor communities
of India began making these designs they used broken cups
and saucers and broken bangles, and ground them into a fine
powder so they could continue this tradition. My mother came
from a poor Dalit family and she often made *rangolis* this way
because her family couldn't afford the expensive rice powders
at the market.

My family would say to me: "You have artistic hands. Go
and make a *rangoli* for the family function." So I found myself
when quite young making many designs on the floor for all
our relatives. After passing my tenth standard at 16, I went

to a college for women in 2001. I studied a diploma in textile design for two years, and took part in college exhibitions. I use lots of flowers in my work because this is integral to my culture. They mark auspicious occasions. Also, we use them to greet and garland our guests, which is a beautiful way of offering natural smells. I love flowers and fruits because of their shades; there is so much variety in nature, so many complexions. I use traditional designs from other states in India like Rajasthan and Gujarat. I've also used imagery from Buddhist monasteries in Darjeeling that I've visited. I'm interested in creating a perfumed beauty.

Since leaving college, I have been quite successful. In 2004 a large and well-known company called Century Mill bought a couple of my designs for their bed sheets and pillow cases, and this year I've had a book of my designs published and the *Maharashtra Times* did a feature about my work. My publishers are confident the book will do well because there is no other book on the market which focuses on the many *rangoli* designs. I'm hoping to have an exhibition of my work in 2007. I have also managed to get work from a company making designs for saris.

I am really committed to my art, and will put it before marriage. I want to be established and stand on my own two feet before I get married. If my family did arrange a proposal, I would ask the family of the man if they were willing to support me as an artist, and if they said no, I would refuse the marriage.

Since working out in the world I have become more conscious of my Buddhist background, because many people at work have asked what my religion is. Once you say you are Buddhist, people assume you are 'downtrodden'. I've never felt I belong to the ex-'Untouchable' class and I don't feel inferior.

Being a Buddhist, I don't feel oppressed. I come from a rich social background. Buddhism isn't just for low caste people; it isn't an inferior religion as some high caste people claim. They often try to argue this because Buddhism was taken on by Ambedkarites and therefore by the 'Untouchables'. My aunt introduced me to Buddhism and told me that the Buddha had all the luxuries of life. She said: look at Prince Siddhartha, the Buddha, he was rich and he went forth to help all human beings. She says I should be a Buddhist artist so that I can create work for the uplift of our people.

I would like to be known as a Dalit artist or a Buddhist artist, and I would like to be able to help my people. So many of them don't have clean lives. They live in unhygienic environments. It's so dirty where they live. They sleep there, they eat there, and many don't go to work. It's very hard to help my people and tell them that you're not supposed to live this way. My dream is to have exhibitions of my work, a manufacturing mill or a textile boutique creating my own designs. This may be a way of helping my people: by employing them in my company, giving them an opportunity to appreciate beauty and earn enough money to improve the quality of their lives.

"I Have Left Hell"

S ignificant moments in the life of a man who tried to emancipate the whole of the Indian nation from the system of caste

Many educated Dalit women who have heard of Dr. Ambedkar will tell you they have their degrees and their jobs because of him. Even the uneducated Dalit woman who has heard of him will tell you he is a great man; he is one of their gods. Uneducated Buddhist women will tell you that he gave them their freedom; he gave them a new rebirth. These Dalit women cannot speak about their lives without praising Ambedkar. He is their saviour. To understand their lives, it is therefore important to know what he fought for, and the struggles he faced in his own life.

Bhimrao Ramji Ambedkar was born on April 14, 1891, in Mhow, central India, into one of the 'Untouchable' castes. Traditionally, people of his caste were forced to live outside the villages, prohibited from entering the temples, not allowed to drink from the public well, beaten for wearing clothes of superior quality, whipped for wearing sandals or socks on their feet. This was the life he was born into. However, the particular circumstances of his family gave him an escape route. A product of what the Indians called the Britishers, Ambedkar reaped the benefit of the British Raj, which gave social mobility to some of the 'Untouchable' castes. His family belonged to the *Mahars*, one of the largest 'Untouchable' castes of India. The *Mahars* and *Matangs* were considered to be among India's martial races, and during the 18th and early 19th centuries the British recruited from these communities for the Indian army, creating a regiment solely for people from the 'Untouchable' castes. They were treated with dignity and respect, and their families were given food, shelter and access to education, which exposed many 'Untouchable' families to a new standard of living.

Ambedkar's family had a military tradition; his grandfather, Maloji, and father, Ramji, both served in the 'Untouchable' regiment. However, two years after Ambedkar was born, in 1893, the regiment was disbanded and 'Untouchables' were no longer recruited. But he was born in time to benefit from his family's service in the army. The British honoured their commitment to all their serving members, re-housing them and giving them jobs. His father was stationed in the district of Satara, and was placed in charge of an army store. The family lived in a military community, and Ambedkar was able to attend a camp school, and then at the age of eight went to an English medium government school. His family had high hopes for him. He was the last and fourteenth child born; only he and six of his siblings survived. His family encouraged him to pursue his education, and his second youngest brother gave up school to work in a factory so that there was enough money for him to continue his studies. He was also noticed by some of his teachers as being exceptionally bright, and even some progressive high caste Hindus supported his education.

Despite the fact that he was married, aged 14, to a nine-year-old girl called Ramabai, he still managed to continue his studies. He entered the Elphinstone College in Mumbai, and his tuition was paid for by the liberal caste Hindu, the Maharaja of Baroda. With the Maharaja's continued assistance, Ambedkar became one of the most highly educated men in India. He graduated with a doctorate in economics from Columbia University, and a PhD in economics from the London School of Economics and Political Science; then he became a barrister in Gray's Inn, London.

Two experiences of 'Untouchability' changed the direction of his life. The first occurred in childhood. His mother died when he was young and his father had to work away from home, so the four youngest children were sent to their aunt's. One day they were invited to visit their father, and had to travel by train. With much enthusiasm the four siblings embarked on their long journey, but when they arrived at the station their father was not there to meet them. A stationmaster took pity on them, but when he realised they were *Mahars*, "His face underwent a sudden change. We could see that he was overpowered by a strange feeling of repulsion."[24] The four children were unable to take a bullock cart to Goregaon, their destination, because word had gone round that the children who were asking for one were 'Untouchables'. Eventually, a caste Hindu agreed for his cart to be used on condition that one of the children drove and he walked behind so as not to be polluted. However, the journey took almost a day, so the driver finally gave in, took the reins and drove. On a stopover at night, the children needed water; they had not drunk anything for more than five hours. The driver suggested that they should lie to the toll collector about their caste. Ambedkar pretended to be a Muslim and spoke in Urdu. But the collector was not stupid. He wanted to know why they had gone without water for so long. Who had kept water from them? Ambedkar couldn't keep up the deception and so he and his three siblings had to sleep without being able to eat, because they needed water to wash down their stale food.

'This incident has an important place in my life. I was a boy of nine when it happened. But it has left an indelible impression on my mind. Before this incident occurred, I knew I was an 'Untouchable' and that 'Untouchables' were subjected to certain indignities and discriminations. For instance, I knew that in school I could not sit in the midst of my class students according to my rank, that I was to sit in a corner by myself.…. this incident gave me a shock such as I never received before, and it made me think about 'Untouchability' which, before this incident happened, was with me a matter of course as it is with many 'Touchables' as well as the 'Untouchables'.'[25]

The second experience came eighteen years later, when he was 27. After he had completed his studies at Columbia University, financed by the Maharaja of Baroda, he was now obliged to serve the state of Baroda. He was employed as a probationer in the accountants' general office, with the intention of becoming Military Secretary of the State. When he arrived at Baroda he had to find somewhere to live but was forced to pass himself off as a Parsi as nobody would give him accommodation because of his caste. As soon as he began his job, his fellow officers would not cooperate. Even the menial workers refused to deal with him; they would throw files at him rather than bring them to his desk.

On the eleventh day, before he left the Parsi inn to go to work, he was disturbed by angry voices and loud footsteps. When he looked to see who it was, he saw a dozen Parsis, each armed with a stick. They were insulted that he had lied about being a Parsi, accused him of polluting the inn, and told him to get out by the evening. Ambedkar, ready to fight this discrimination, turned to his caste Hindu friends. One said: "If you come to my home my servants will leave." And the other, a Brahmin who had converted to Christianity, politely told him that he would have to consult his wife before he could invite him to stay.

Finally, Ambedkar broke down. He had no friends and nobody to turn to. He couldn't face going back to his office, he couldn't return to the inn, and there was only one train to Mumbai that evening. He took refuge in a public garden and sat there for five hours waiting for his train. He wondered what life must be like for the millions of 'Untouchables' in India. If he, with a PhD, was treated like this, what about the millions who were uneducated? Ambedkar had believed that if he was educated he would be treated like a human being. After all, in America and in the United Kingdom his caste had not mattered. "My five years of stay in Europe and America had completely wiped out of my mind any consciousness that I was an 'Untouchable' and that an 'Untouchable', wherever he went in India, was a problem to himself and to others."[26]

But his experience in Baroda gave him a resounding awakening. On November 17, 1917, the day he left to go back to Mumbai, he made a commitment to himself to work for the benefit of his people, and soon afterwards began his campaign of political and social activism. In 1919 he gave evidence before the Southborough Committee, demanding political rights for the Depressed Classes of India and highlighting the plight of the 'Untouchables'. It was this that brought the issue of caste actively into the consideration of the political movements of the country.

Ambedkar resumed his studies in England, was called to the Bar in 1923 and then returned to India in 1924 to set up a legal practice at the Mumbai High Court as well as launching his public career as a social worker, politician, writer and educationalist. In 1926 he was appointed to the Bombay Legislative Assembly, along with another Dalit leader from Gujarat. For the next thirty years he worked as a legislator while also leading demonstrations, giving lectures, holding sit-ins, and negotiating with Hindu leaders and the British government for the basic human rights of the Dalits. He argued that the 'Untouchables' were humans, and therefore should have civil and political rights in his country. He also fought for the emancipation of the peasant and working classes.

There were several significant events that marked his political career. The first was the struggle for the rights of the 'Untouchables' to drink water from a public well. The municipality of a small town in the Konkan, Mahad, had declared all public property open to all castes. However, some caste Hindus managed to argue in court that the tank for water was private property. In 1927, on 20th March, Ambedkar and other leaders such as Anantrao Chitre led a crowd of 1,500 Untouchables from a political conference they were attending to drink from the public tank in Mahad. News of this action spread, and furious caste Hindus came and beat up hundreds of 'Untouchables' who had dared to drink water from the tank. The caste Hindus then ceremonially purified the tank with five products of the cow: dung, urine, milk, curds and clarified butter.

This incident became national news and for several months afterwards there was much rioting and political organising throughout the State of Maharashtra. The tank was sealed, and Ambedkar and 15,000 of his Dalit followers returned eight months later to reopen it. But with the careful negotiation of the British, Ambedkar agreed not to go ahead and reopen it. Instead, two days later, on 25th December, in front of 15,000 'Untouchables', he led a ceremonial burning of the *Manusmriti*, claiming that the text was a symbol of injustice whereby his people had been crushed for centuries. He had the support of some Brahmins for this action. Although many people in his movement were against Brahmins and other high caste people being involved in the political and social struggle, Ambedkar made it clear to his followers that his fight was against Brahminism, not Brahmins.

Ambedkar was determined to create a new constitutional framework for India. His fight for separate electorates brought about the famous Poona Pact between himself and Mahatma

Gandhi. Ambedkar wanted separate electorates for the Scheduled Castes, as they were a social and religious minority. Lord Simon, the chairman of the Commission to investigate Indian claims for self-government, was sympathetic but gave in to the pressure of Gandhi's Congress Party. But in 1932 the British Prime Minister, Ramsay MacDonald, created 78 seats in the Central Legislature for Dalits, and moved that they should be given a double vote. However, MacDonald's plans were opposed by Gandhi. Although he had been arrested and was in prison, he found a way of protesting: he went on hunger strike. He objected to the provision of separate electorates for the 'Untouchables' because, in his view, it would divide the Indian nation. He announced a fast unto death if the plan went ahead. Ambedkar had no choice but to give in. Realising that if Gandhi died, thousands of Dalits would be killed, he compromised and agreed to replace separate electorates with reservations in joint electorates according to which four 'Untouchable' candidates would be selected, and the number of seats allocated to 'Untouchables' doubled to 148. This came to be known as the Poona Pact of September 24, 1932. Ambedkar was saddened by this compromise and Vijay Mankar quotes him as saying: "I'm feeling as if I bought a very good fruit from the British, a very juicy fruit indeed. Gandhi and his followers took the fruit from me, they peeled the fruit, squeezed all the juice, drank all the juice, and they have thrown the rind in my face."[27]

In 1935, at the Yeola Conference for Depressed Classes, Ambedkar created a national stir among caste Hindus. "The explosion took place at Yeola on October 13, 1935 and it rocked Hindu India in a way that the burning of the *Manusmriti* had not done."[28] Ambedkar publicly denounced Hinduism. Believing that it created an unjust society, he said he would leave the Hindu fold and find another religion. He encouraged Dalit leaders to consider their religious identity, and told them that if they wanted to gain self-respect they should change their religion. He argued that because the disabilities of the 'Untouchable' castes arose from their belonging to the Hindu religion, if they wanted to emancipate themselves from casteism, it was time for them to sever all connection with Hinduism. He began to seek another religion through following which the 'Untouchables' could gain self-respect.

However, he had not given up on politics. He remained politically active in the following years, setting up a succession of political parties designed to help his cause. With the aim of uniting the lower classes, which made up the majority of the Indian population, in 1936 he founded the Independent Labour Party, or ILP, which had a strong working class identity. However, this broad alliance proved to be unsuccessful. Meanwhile, the British wanted to know how Ambedkar could represent the Scheduled Castes when he had no Scheduled Caste organisation behind him. After much deliberation, he wound down the ILP and in 1942 founded the Scheduled Caste Federation as an all-India political party. Unlike the ILP it was successful in achieving a national representation of Dalits across the country. However, it was unable to represent the broad masses of the working class and peasants as the ILP had done, and after a time it was split by factionalism. It finally collapsed shortly after Ambedkar's death. Ambedkar's final attempt at creating a party that would speak for all the oppressed sections of India society was the Republican Party of India. In fact, he didn't live to set it up himself; it was established in 1957, a year after his death, based on the draft of a constitution that he had written before he died. He had hoped that all these organisations would bring about the end of a caste-based identity, but sadly none of them achieved this, and the Republican Party of India today is split into several factions, and controlled by the *Mahar* community.

However, Ambedkar did achieve a very notable success in the field of politics. After the British left India in 1947,

Pandit Nehru, the first Prime Minister of India, brought Ambedkar into his Constituent Assembly as Law Minister and appointed him as chairman of the drafting committee of the Indian Constitution in 1947. In this capacity he took the lead in framing the Constitution of India, which laid the basis for the social transformation of India. On January 26, 1950, 'Untouchability' was made illegal, and Ambedkar instituted reservations in public services for the Dalit community and other minorities as part of the Constitution.

"Never in 5,000 years did we have such a dramatic change in this country. We got the right to education, the right to participate in decision-making by vote, the right to citizenship, the right to religious freedom and equality before the law, the right of participation by means of reservations, and a new life and new identity. The movement of the oppressed people of India got the social and constitutional recognition of India, which the *Sudras* and the *Atysudras* (outcastes) had never had before." [29]

Ambedkar was hailed by some as the modern Manu, who gave India a new democratic regime. Despite this accolade, a year later, after the Constitution had been established, he resigned in disappointment. His Hindu Code Bill, a charter of women's rights in a new free India, which tried to bring about civil rights for all women, arguing for full rights in marriage and property, was not supported. Also, he realised that he had only ensured equality for the Dalit community in Constitutional Law. In society and in economic terms they still suffered inequality. He believed that this inequality of caste had been sanctioned by Hinduism. Since Hinduism sanctioned caste, if the Dalits remained Hindu they could not escape caste or reconstruct society. Dr. Ambedkar said, "To remain in Hinduism and to attempt to abolish the caste system is like sweetening poison." His message to the Dalit community was that if they really wanted equality and dignity, they would have to renounce Hinduism and accept Buddhism. Unless they threw out the scriptures and the gods and goddesses they wouldn't be free of caste. He argued that because caste was a social phenomenon which had no reality, but merely existed as a notion in the mind, to get rid of caste the 'Untouchables' had to change their minds. Buddhism was the best religion to convert to, he thought, because Buddhism was about the reformation of the mind. Ambedkar wrote: "The greatest thing that the Buddha has done is to tell the world that the world cannot be reformed except by the reformation of the mind of man, and the mind of the world."[30]

On the basis of this belief he led one of the biggest conversions to another religion ever held on a single day. On October 14, 1956, in Nagpur, he and approximately five hundred thousand white-clad women, men and children, from all over Maharashtra and a few other states, took *deeksha* (conversion). He said to the crowd: "Those who want to convert please stand." And it is reported that the entire crowd rose at this moment. They watched their leader take the three refuges and five precepts from the most senior Buddhist monk in India, Chandramani Maha Thera, and then witnessed Ambedkar recite 22 vows he had written himself, which included the vow:

"I shall have no faith in Brahma, Vishnu and Mahesh nor shall I worship them. I renounce Hinduism, which is harmful for humanity and impedes the advancement and development of humanity because it is based on inequality, and adopt Buddhism as my religion."

Minutes later the crowd followed suit and took *deeksha* from Ambedkar. When Ambedkar was asked how he felt, it is reported that he said: "I am happy. I am ecstatic! I have left hell. This is how I feel."[31] His disciples are also reported to have said: "We feel free, no longer Hindus, no longer in the caste system, no longer 'Untouchables'."[32] They had converted because Ambedkar had told them to, because they had great faith in him. Most knew nothing about Buddhism at all; their motivation was to escape the caste into which they had been born, to change their karma and have a new 'rebirth' in this lifetime.

In the following five years, 2.5 million people in the State of Maharashtra converted to Buddhism. Ambedkar's dream had been to convert the whole of India; thus, he believed, casteism would be entirely wiped out. Perhaps he was right but, unfortunately, he did not live long enough to see his dream fulfilled, or even to convert the entire Dalit community in India. His life was so short. He was found dead on December 6, 1956, just seven weeks after the conversion ceremony. He only managed to convert his own caste, the *Mahar* caste, and a few thousand other people from other states of India, to Buddhism. His dream had been to travel round the whole of India and convert all the 'Untouchables'. But it was the *Mahar* people who were left with his legacy. Since the conversion, most of the *Mahars* have converted, but a few people from other castes have followed suit. And so, because it is predominantly the *Mahars* who have converted, in India today Buddhism has become virtually synonymous with 'Untouchability', and some scholars, including Buddhists, perceive it merely as a political and social act.

It isn't surprising that the authenticity of the conversion to Buddhism has been called into question. "Ambedkar's followers had received a terrible shock. They had been Buddhist only seven weeks, and now their leader, in whom their trust was total, and on whose guidance in the difficult days ahead they had been relying, had been snatched away. Poor and illiterate as the vast majority of them were, and faced by the unrelenting hostility of the caste Hindus, they did not know which way to turn, and there was a possibility that the whole movement of conversion to Buddhism would come to a halt or even collapse."[33]

Ambedkar had believed that teachers from all over the world would pour resources into this new Buddhist society, but only a few monks came and they only taught the people how to give alms and chant the precepts. After Ambedkar's death it was assumed that the Buddhist Society of India, which he had founded in 1955, and his political parties, would teach the people about the new way of living. But politics dominated the scene, and there were few teachers who could teach people about Buddhism.

Most second and third generation Buddhist families in Maharashtra call themselves Buddhist but still follow the Hindu gods and celebrate Hindu festivals. Many only know the Buddha's name and the chanting of the five precepts. The majority are ethnic Buddhists, born into Buddhism, but having little or no idea of what it means to be a Buddhist or live a Buddhist life. For many of them Ambedkar is Buddha. He is a god. "My grandparents converted to Buddhism only because Babasaheb told them that they should not die as Hindus. That was how all the people of their generation converted to Buddhism. But after Babasaheb there was nobody to teach the people how to live a Buddhist life. So they all converted but still worshipped and followed Hindu culture."[34]

The part of Ambedkar's legacy that has changed the lives of many castes of the Dalit community, not just the *Mahars*, is the provision of education. In 1945 he founded the People's Education Society, which started a number of colleges in Bombay for the Dalits and other communities. Many people today will say: "It is because of Ambedkar that I am a lawyer, a doctor, in business, an administrator. It is because of him that I am educated."

The political parties and the social work movement came to the Dalit community's rescue after Ambedkar's death. In 1957 the Republican Party of India was formed on the basis of the Constitution that Ambedkar had drafted before he died, and it continued his movement in the direction of politics and social work. And the Dalit Panthers were founded 16 years later; the name was inspired by the Black Panthers in America, and they took up the basic issues of caste, economics, and social welfare.

Both these movements gave the Dalits a public voice in India right up to the 1970s, and they formed the basis of the Bahujan Samaj Party, which was founded by Kanshi Ram in 1984. By bringing together the Dalit and the *Sudra* castes under one banner, Kanshi Ram hoped that his party would be the governing party of India by 2004. Then, he said, he would march towards the dream of Dr. Ambedkar and Buddhism, preparing the Dalit and *Sudra* communities to embrace Buddhism in India in the Golden Jubilee year of Ambedkar's conversion in 2006. Unfortunately, he fell ill and died on October 9, 2006, before any of his dreams were realised. However, the Bahujan Samaj Party does have some influence. It is the only Dalit political party to be recognised as a national party in India. It now ranks as the fourth national party, and is led by Mayawati, who is the first Dalit woman to be Chief Minister of a state in India. Mayawati told the masses in Nagpur in October 2006, that she would not convert to Buddhism till she achieves her goal of being the first Dalit Prime Minister of India. She believes that then the entire Dalit community will follow her. On May 11, 2007, she took complete control of Uttar Pradesh, under her new slogan "Haati nahin Ganesh hai. Brahma, Vishnu, Mahesh hai" (it is not elephant but Lord Ganesh, symbolising all gods and communities) which caught the attention of upper castes.

Whether she will be able to carry out the whole of the Ambedkar dream of conversion, remains to be seen. But she has most definitely blazed his trail, by creating a social mix and including the upper castes in her election platform. Those organisations spreading the word of Buddhism still struggle, because it is viewed as the salvation for the Dalit community.

The Buddhist Society of India train men to conduct Buddhist ceremonies, lead rituals and organise programmes on significant dates of Ambedkar's life, and the Dalai Lama, who settled in India in 1959, praised Ambedkar's work. Ten years later, S.N. Goenka came back to his ancestral home from Burma and reintroduced the Buddhist meditation practice of *vipassana*. Some people saw this as a breakthrough because he introduced Buddhism to all the castes of India, taking it out of the *Mahar* ghetto. In 2006 he said, at a national programme in Mumbai, that he believed *vipassana* could solve all India's problems because it is about changing the mind.

But the spiritual group which has perhaps had most impact on the families which converted in 1956 is the Trailokya Bauddha Mahasangha Sahayak Gana (TBMSG). It was founded in 1979 by the venerable Urgyen Sangharakshita (founder of the Friends of the Western Buddhist Order or FWBO), who had been in India at the time of the great conversion and knew Dr. Ambedkar. Some 23 years later one of his disciples, Dhammachari Lokamitra, came to India and visited some of Sangharakshita's friends; and he saw that the people who had converted to Buddhism, lacking any direction or knowledge, were hungry for Buddhist teachings. In response to this need, the FWBO expanded its order by founding TBMSG in India, as part of a worldwide order with members in Europe, the Americas, Australia, New Zealand and South Africa.

TBMSG has played an important role in the Dalit community's exposure to the teachings of the Buddha. It has encouraged spiritual development through meditation and retreats and contributed to improving the quality of life of the Dalits through its education, health and social projects. Although TBMSG's work has been mainly in the *Mahar* community, during the past few years it has begun to work in other states of India, working with other Dalits and some OBCs to empower themselves with the help of Buddhism. "When TBMSG came to India in 1979 it was like a bright light for the Dalit community, who had been blind to Buddhism for 23 years. Before joining TBMSG, I was working with the Buddhist Society of India and my experience was sad. There were no systematic programmes for the people, nothing constructive to help the people learn about the Dhamma. TBMSG changed all of that by providing proper Dhamma study, retreats and effective meditation training. It gave a positive way forward for the people."[35]

During the past five years a collection of Buddhist individuals and groups from different traditions (Dhammakranti) have come together to teach Buddhism to different castes throughout India. They run a yearly programme called DhammaYatra, in which they travel around and give talks in cities, villages and remote areas; it is estimated that this has touched the lives of over five hundred thousand people.

However the Buddhist Society is also a strong presence and has been setting up retreats throughout India, to help deal with the alcoholism in the Dalit communities.

But there is still much to be done if the entre Dalit community in India is to be emancipated. The vast majority are uneducated and are still slaves in the Hindu system: "Most Dalits continue to live in extreme poverty, without land or opportunities for better employment or education. With the exception of a minority who have benefited from India's policy of quotas in education and government jobs, Dalits are relegated to the most menial of tasks, as manual scavengers, removers of human waste and dead animals, leather workers, street sweepers and cobblers. Dalit children make up the majority of those sold into bondage to pay off debts to upper caste creditors."[36]

And it is the Dalit woman who suffers most in today's society. Ambedkar wanted all Dalit women to be educated, and liberated from Hinduism. In fact, some argue that he was able to achieve so much in his life because of his two wives. His first, Ramabai, who gave birth to five children, with only the first son surviving, supported him wholeheartedly in his work. It was to his great regret that she died aged 40 in 1935, before he could give her and his family the attention and support that he wanted to give them. In 1948 he married Dr. Savita Kabir, who was a Brahmin. She was a medical doctor and cared for him during the last eight years of his life, so he could prepare and conduct the great conversion. This second marriage was in line with his belief that to destroy casteism, people must have inter-caste marriages.

His dreams of a Buddhist India, of the formation of a casteless society and democracy, of an end to the caste economy, his dreams that Dalits should become the governing class of India, and that every Dalit woman and her children should be educated, have still not been realised. But the mass conversion proved that those who became ethnic Buddhists, even if Buddhist in name only, could stand up for themselves and break down barriers. More people from the ex-*Mahar* community are to be seen in places of responsibility and power in the professional fields than any other caste in the Dalit community.

The Buddhists have prioritised education and have at all costs tried to educate at least one or two of their children, though mainly boys. But the majority are still poor, living in slums and in the villages, and now they are at risk of losing reserved places in education and the public services, as recent governments have set about privatising education and many public services.

Ambedkar's life was full of ironies. For an 'Untouchable' to achieve all that he did at the beginning of the 20th century was unheard of. He spent his whole life campaigning against Hinduism and Brahminism but all his benefactors and some of his close friends were Brahmins. Even his name is ironic: he became the most celebrated leader of the Dalits, and yet he was named after a Brahmin. His last name should have been Sankpal, but his father, wanting to move away from any connotations of 'Untouchabililty', decided to name him after his ancestral village, Ambavade. But, moved by the kindness of a Brahmin teacher called Ambedkar who had shown pity to his son by providing lunch for him every day because of his long walk to school, he changed his mind and registered his son's last name as 'Ambedkar' in honour of his teacher. It is ironic, too, that Ambedkar, born an 'Untouchable' into one of the many castes by which every caste Hindu feared being polluted, was the man who gave India its Constitution. Although Ambedkar once claimed he was the most hated person in India, 'a snake in the Hindus' garden', statues of him, clad in a city gent's suit, holding the Constitution under his left arm and pointing with his right hand, stand boldly outside educational and governmental institutions throughout the country. His statue has also been raised in Dalit villages throughout India. Of course there has been some backlash, with caste Hindus garlanding the statues with *chappals* (sandals), which is one of the worst insults you can give an Indian, because the *chappal* is worn on the lowest part of the body.

Ambedkar is affectionately and respectfully remembered by his followers as Babasaheb, and instead of using the Hindu greeting 'Namaste', the new Buddhists greet each other with 'Jai Bhim!' ('Victory to Bhimrao!') "He is hailed as a beacon for people fighting against the Hindu caste system and other forms of oppression, including gender discrimination. Needless to say, he is considered an enemy by those who want to perpetuate the Hindu caste system. He has almost become a poster boy for the major political parties in India, since they cannot ignore two hundred million people – and voters – from the lowest strata of Indian society."[37]

Ambedkar's mission still has a long way to go. But through politics, education, social work and spiritual work, many Dalit women and men are trying to maintain his legacy. He would have most definitely been proud of Mayawati, and welcomed the social mix that the Bahujun Samaj Party are now advocating, "We Dalits need to become visible. We need to create an aesthetic, including literature, politics, arts and culture. We need social recognition in society. We need to give voices to the victims of the oppression of Hindu culture."[38] Ambedkar's dream must live on through the Dalit woman, because it is she who passes the culture on to the children. It is she whose identity is still tied up in Hindu festivals. It is she who is still left at home to do her domestic duties. The Dalit man needs to realise that the education of his wife and his daughters is imperative to the mission. Otherwise, conversion to Buddhism is nothing more than an exercise of changing a name – "Hinduism" to "Buddhism" – with the laws of Manu still imprinted on the minds of those who are oppressed by those same laws. If the people of the Dalit community are to gain emancipation, caste must be wiped out from the whole of India. The Dalit community must liberate their minds from caste. As Ambedkar said, "Caste is a notion, a state of mind."

Conversion

Ambedkar's daughter
A servant of the Buddha
Dalit heroine

I was born in 1942 in the town of Nagpur, which is now famous in the Buddhist world as the place where Dr. Babasaheb Ambedkar led the mass conversion of 'Untouchable' people to Buddhism. Before this conversion you could say that life for the 'Untouchables' was worse than the lives of animals. We had no human rights and no humanity was shown to my community. We were restricted from being involved in education, trade and finance. We could not earn money or own land and there were very few sources for our livelihood. All we could do was serve the caste Hindus. We 'Untouchables' had a miserable lot. This was how I began my life.

My parents are from the *Mahar* caste. This means 'Untouchable'. I am an only child. My mother worked as a servant to the high caste Hindus and my father worked in a cotton mill, doing labouring work, along with all the other *Mahar* people who were employed by the Brahmins. We lived in a corrugated iron hut in the slum area. I was quite fortunate because my father was part of the social movement of Dr. Ambedkar, which was trying to give the *Mahar* people their human rights. He told me many stories about Babasaheb, and said that if he sent me to school outside the slum, I could get a scholarship because of Babasaheb's hard work. He told me that in his childhood he had had very little education, because he had to work for the high caste Hindus, and that all the *Mahar* people in his village were servants.

He managed to get me into a government school so I could do my primary education. They couldn't refuse *Mahar* children so I was lucky. Every class had a maximum of three *Mahar* students. We always had to sit behind the Brahmins and other caste Hindus, and the teachers didn't care much about us and gave all their attention to the other children, but my father taught me at home, so I didn't lag behind. My father also told me I was fortunate that he had moved away from the village, because many children like me were slaves of the high caste people. But he was going to make sure that he followed the philosophy of Babasaheb and try to give me an education.

I was 13 when the conversion happened. Three months before that great day my father went to a meeting and then came home and explained to me that something important was going to happen in our lives. He said: whatever Babasaheb says, we will follow. Whatever he asks the *Mahar* people to do, it will be to our benefit. My mother didn't understand, but she had faith in my father and faith in Ambedkar, and did as she was told. I remember the days leading up to the conversion very clearly. My slum just grew rapidly, with people coming from all over Mahasrashtra. The *Mahar* people had no money but still they came. Some took three or four days to walk to Nagpur. My father informed me that many of them had sold everything they owned so they could come to the conversion and wear the colour white. There were over 200 people camped around my hut. It was the same everywhere in the slum: people camping, burning fires and singing, everyone smiling and very happy.

On the 14th of October, thousands of us lined up in pairs and walked to the *deeksha bhumi* (conversion place), a big area in the middle of Nagpur. We walked calmly chanting the slogan:

"Dr. Ambedkar is telling us to change our religion. Come into Buddhism today." We were all joyful. There were lakhs and lakhs of people. I can still see Dr. Ambedkar on the stage with his wife, along with some *bhikkhus*. My heart is dancing as if it all happened yesterday. I can see Babasaheb's face now. I was prepared to follow whatever he said because my father had promised that our lives would change. I witnessed him take the five traditional precepts: "I undertake to abstain from taking life; I undertake to abstain from taking the not given; I undertake to abstain from sexual misconduct; I undertake to abstain from false speech; I undertake to abstain from taking intoxicants." And then I remember him reading out a long list of vows to do with throwing out the gods. He explained that we should not worship the Hindu gods any more, or do what the Brahmin people told us to do. He made it clear that the Buddha was not a god but a human being. I didn't know what all the vows meant, but I knew they were important because I looked up at my parents and saw tears in their eyes. I looked around and many people were crying. And then my parents repeated the precepts and vows along with everybody else.

I remember Bahasaheb questioning the crowd. He said things like: "Who taught you that you are 'Untouchable' because of what you did in your previous life? Who told you that this is why you have to drag dead animals and dead people out of the village? Who told you that this is because of your bad karma in a previous life? It's all lies. Educate your mind. You must educate yourself, your women and your children. I'm educated, but still people treat me badly. How do you expect people to treat you well if you're not educated?"

On the way home, my father explained to me that I was not to believe anything that the Hindu religion taught me. I wasn't to worship any Hindu gods or do what the Brahmins told me. I was not to confuse Hinduism with Buddhism. I returned home on that day feeling proud to be a Buddhist. As soon as we entered our home, my father cleared it of any Hindu images. He and many others in the village threw out the gods and burned them. The next day I went back to school and the Brahmin teachers laughed at all the *Mahar* children: "Look at them. They think they are special now because they are Buddhists. They think they are higher than us Brahmins. You will always be from the *Mahar* caste. If you don't have money to pay for your exams, just write '*Mahar*' in your file and we won't want to touch your money." When I told my father about this, he was furious, and said: "Never ever write '*Mahar*' again. You are a Buddhist." He was able to find money for my exams.

The day Babasaheb died was so sad. I was at school, and I heard two teachers whispering: "Dr. Ambedkar is dead." I didn't believe them, because since the conversion the teachers had made nasty jokes about my community and Dr. Ambedkar. Then an hour later someone came to our school and asked the head teacher to close it for the rest of the day. He announced that Dr. Ambedkar was dead. I went home with tears in my eyes. When I reached my home the whole slum area was weeping loudly. My father hugged me and said: "Our father has died."

Nobody ate that day. On the day of the funeral most of the men went to Mumbai, where it was to take place, and the women and children left behind proceeded to Kasturchand Park, and we cried and paid our respects. Many of my community were confused; they didn't know if they were Hindu or Buddhist. Some of them began praying to the Hindu gods again. Nobody knew anything about Buddhism. The whole community was left without a clear direction, in disarray, and many people returned to the Hindu way of life, worshipping the gods and believing themselves to be inferior.

My father was sad and confused after Bahasaheb's death,

because many of the political leaders who had worked with him fought among themselves, and his Republican party split into many different parties. Also, there was nobody to teach us about Buddhism. I was lucky: my father had a book called *The Buddha and His Dhamma*, by Dr. Ambedkar. It was the only thing my community had after his death. But many people couldn't read. What were we to do? I remember hearing the Buddha's teachings and about how the Buddha believed in the equality of all people. This was a turning point in my life. I had never heard anyone talk about the *Mahars* as being equal to others. Although I grew up in the city, all of us living in the slums were still oppressed.

I also realised how important it was to be a woman after hearing stories about the Buddha. Someone told a story that always stays with me. It is about King Prasenajit, who was sitting with the Buddha when a servant burst in on their meeting. The man fell down before the Buddha's feet and said: "Queen Mallika has just given birth to a girl." The Buddha looked at the king and saw that he looked extremely ill. He asked what was wrong, and when he realised that the king was upset that his new child was a girl, he said: "Don't be sorry. She may be better offspring than a male child. She may even give birth to a boy who will do great deeds."

My father told me about the good things Babasaheb said about women. He warned me to be careful whom I married because Babasaheb had said: "If your father, brother or husband comes home drunk, don't open the door. If you open it he will beat you, and if you keep it closed he'll beat the door. So you may as well keep it closed." Unfortunately, many women have ignored this advice.

I left school in 1960, and my father applied for a scholarship for me. Ambedkar had made this possible because of the reserved places for all *Mahar* people. This was part of his legacy. He made it law that the government must give some college places to the ex 'Untouchable' community. So I was able to have a proper university education and graduate with a degree. I married in my 20s and my husband was kind. However, when we first married we made a big mistake. We were unable to find a house to live in, so we lied about our caste. I still regret this today. We never did it again. Living a lie was so painful. I saw how the *Mahar* people were treated so badly and I couldn't say anything, otherwise we would be found out.

But I became part of a group that campaigned to change the name of a university in Aurangabad to Dr. Ambedkar. The government agreed to our request but the Brahmins and other caste Hindus kicked up a huge fuss, to the extent that there were big fights. They refused to serve us in the shops if we greeted them with 'Jai Bhim!' Some even threatened to kill us if we continued to use this greeting. Some Hindus refused to give us work, and there was much bloodshed during our ten years' fight. The government was so scared that they didn't put the name change into effect. So I took part in huge demonstrations. The police often threw large rocks at us, and some even fired into the crowd. I was sent to jail twice for being part of the demonstrations. Some years later the government gave in and now in Aurangabad we have a university named after our leader.

During this same time I heard about Buddhist meetings happening in Nagpur. They were being held by the TBMSG. It was fantastic; it was the first time that I had received any formal teaching about Buddhism. I went to meetings when I could, and began going on retreats in 1982. These changed my life, and I began to find a new confidence about being a Buddhist and letting go of my old identity as a *Mahar*. In 1997 I took another *deeksha*. I was invited to join a Buddhist Order.

I was ordained into the TBMSG, along with one other woman, Vimalasuri. We were the first two women in India to join this order. Converting a second time is a big responsibility. I must help other lost Buddhists who are still suffering from the effects of receiving no help when their families converted 50 years ago. TBMSG has only reached a fraction of the Dalit community who need to learn about Buddhism.

Life still continues to be a struggle today for my community. One of my daughters graduated from medical school, and they tried to fail her on her practical. They told her the day before the practical exam: "You're the first *Mahar* student we've had. What makes you think you will pass?" The next day they failed her. But it didn't deter her; she appeared for it again and passed. I complained to the college. I told them that my daughter had every right to be there. She was a guest of the government; the college weren't paying for her.

Through Ambedkar's teachings, and the Buddha's teachings, I am learning to love myself every day. I am fortunate to have converted twice to Buddhism. I am also fortunate to have grown up in a city, because there are still people in the 21st century who live like animals in the villages, owing to the oppression of Brahministic and Hindu philosophies. People still believe in the *Vedas*, and some even try to live in accordance with the *Manusmriti*.

> *Most important day*
> *His birth - Deeksha conversion*
> *His death – Fated day*

I am now 75 years old but the exact number of years has not been recorded in my mind. My birthday has never been celebrated so the years are not so important, but the life I have lived is. I was born in a small village in the district of Satara. We 'Untouchables' all lived in one section of the village and we were punished if we ever crossed the boundary without permission. I couldn't even buy things in the shops which were on the border between the lower caste and the higher caste communities. The high caste people sometimes refused to serve me, and they never let me touch any of their goods.

I was married when I was around nine years old. I don't know how old my husband was but he worked for the railway service so he may have been 16 or 17. I can imagine the years as I have watched my own children grow and have learned to tell ages this way. I was still very small when I married; I hadn't even begun to menstruate. All the saris provided were too big for me, so my mother had to make me something to wear. I was too young to understand what was happening. What I remember is that I lost my family and my home, and went to live in a stranger's home. But I was fortunate because my husband was an only child and so his parents were glad to receive a daughter; they gave me great love and affection.

I moved to Mumbai and lived in one of the old prisons for freedom fighters that the British had built when India was fighting for Independence. My father and mother-in-law, my husband and I all lived in a prison cell. There were three floors with 15 cells on each floor. We had no lights, no toilets, and had to go downstairs into the courtyard for water to cook and bathe with. Look around for yourself; this is where my children and grandchildren all grew up. After my menses began, I gave birth to my first child, and four more children followed, so we were four adults and five small children all huddled up in this cell. There was nowhere to escape to for peace and quiet, because many people lived in the hallways of the buildings. See how they all drink and gamble outside. It was no different then.

I live in the district of Worli in Mumbai, where there are many factories. It's a place where Dr. Ambedkar came to speak to the people. I first heard about him after the birth of my first child, when I was about 15. He was giving a three-day conference near where I lived, and the whole family went to the public area and heard him give lectures. We all began to attend his programmes, and I was so close to him once that I managed to put a coin in his pocket for good luck. There were many meetings in the year leading up to the conversion. I wasn't able to attend the ceremony in Nagpur, and was hoping to take *deeksha* from Babasaheb in Mumbai. He had arranged a date after the Nagpur event to do a *deeksha* in the city where he lived. But he didn't live long enough to return. He died before my family and many others could convert.

I took my *deeksha* from an English man in robes. I know now that his name was Sangharakshita. I heard that he had been very kind to the people in Nagpur in the days after Babasaheb died. He gave us the 22 vows and this is how my whole family became Buddhist. My eldest son was eight and the other four were still small. My in-laws and husband were all very happy because we had received a rebirth from the Hindu religion to a new religion, Buddhism. We had grown up to believe that we could only change our caste through death. If we served the Brahmins then perhaps we would get a better rebirth next time around.

This day was the most important day in our lives, although I was sad not to have received *deeksha* from Babasaheb himself. We left all our gods and goddesses behind us. I received the news of his death on the radio. I was so shocked that I didn't even look to find my children playing in the hallway outside my home. I just left the house in a daze with my in-laws and husband and went to Dadar in the hope of seeing his body. So many people were outside his house that you couldn't turn your head sideways. On the day of his funeral, people were wailing, and some were trying to jump into the burning pyre. It was a very sad day indeed. The crowds were so large that I wasn't able to return to my house. I had to wait for the moon to rise; that's when the masses began to leave. I'll always remember that fateful day.

> *We have converted*
> *Because we want to be human*
> *Now is the good life*

In 1944 I heard Babasaheb speak at a programme. I was only 13, but I remember him saying that he wouldn't die a Hindu. This message remained fixed in my mind forever. But what did he mean? How could this be? Twelve years later, I converted to Buddhism under his guidance. The conversion took us out of the pollution of Hinduism. I felt that I was taken from a very bad situation into a good life. My family weren't recognised as human beings in the Hindu religion. We wanted to have our identity as human beings, and we saw that Buddhism could give us this.

At the time of conversion Babasaheb said: "I am free from hell; this is my rebirth." This had a strong impact on me, and all the people around me. When I recited the 22 vows for the first time I didn't understand them at all, but when I began to work for the Buddhist movement they began to make sense. They reminded me of my life in the past, when I was living a polluted 'Untouchable' life. I couldn't drink water from the common well in my village. I couldn't even wear sandals because I was 'Untouchable'. In fact, I was beaten up by the high caste people for wearing sandals in my village. I salute Dr. Ambedkar for giving me this great religion, Buddhism. When I began to understand the 22 vows, I realised what a great person he was.

I was living in Mumbai after the conversion, near the red light district, in the place where he had given many famous speeches. When the news came to Mumbai that he had died, nobody wanted to believe it. People were beating each other up, slapping each other and shouting: "This is false news, this is an awful rumour." I had a small baby only 15 days old but, not thinking, I left my newborn at home alone and went outside to tell the people to stop beating each other because the news had been confirmed. It was a dark night. Nobody cooked in their homes, no lights were burning. All the 350 flats in the block I lived in were in mourning.

I was unable to attend the funeral because of my small baby, but Babasaheb's body was brought to his residence in Dadar, and I went and paid my tribute to him there. I lost my mind. I kept crying. I couldn't think of anything to say to him, so I put my head on his feet and wept. I had seen him twice, but I never spoke to him directly out of respect. But in 1952 he had some elections in Mumbai. At that time the Hindu people were beating up the Dalit people, and so some of us went to tell him about it. He said: "Why are you telling me? You should be ashamed of yourselves. You have to fight, don't come and cry." He said: "If someone beats you up, you're not supposed to sit quietly and put up with that beating. This is what you have done for so many years. You must do something different, not just cry and complain." This meeting was the moment that made me realise I must get up and fight for my basic human rights, but it took me another four years to find the courage.

I began working in the Ambedkarite movement in 1956, immediately after the conversion. I decided to be an active participant in his movement for spreading the Dhamma and uplifting women's lives. I realised that we women were the members of the family who worshipped the gods most, so I needed to let them know what Buddhism was. I helped families to remove Hindu gods from their homes, and taught them that it was the Buddha we were following now. I even threw out my own precious silver gods.

I began to help the children from the Buddhist community with their education. I helped make school materials available for the poor. Babasaheb had said: "Educate yourself, be united and fight for your rights." He really wanted women to be educated because he believed that if the woman in the family was educated, she could make sure the whole family was educated. There is a proverb in Marathi: "The one who swings the cradle is the one who can uplift the child." By education you can nourish the family. Women have the power to convert the whole world. Dr. Ambedkar said: "If women step forward, they can bring about a revolution in the world."

I'm a follower of Ambedkar because of his thoughts and the life he has given me as a human being. After conversion I felt very strongly about never bowing down to any gods in my life again. I only wanted to follow the path of the Buddha, the path of peace. But I don't believe in just closing my eyes, meditating and sitting quietly. I believe in getting up, going out and giving compassion. It is my duty, as someone who converted fifty years ago, to spread the Dhamma. This was Ambedkar's dream. There are too many people calling themselves Buddhists who pursue politics because they think they will get money and a big house. I feel these people have not taken his message seriously.

I have often been asked to stand for elections, but I have refused each time because I don't want to become corrupted. To really help society, to help the Dalit situation without selfishness and greed, I cannot align myself to a political party. There is too much distraction, corruption and bribery. Many Dalits have made themselves educated, earning large sums of money, and have forgotten Dr. Ambedkar's dream: the conversion of the entire Dalit community to Buddhism. He also wanted unity among the Dalit community. It is mainly only the *Mahar* caste who have converted, and we are most definitely not united as a community.

Since October 14, 1956 I have fought for the end of casteism, the end of Hinduism, the end of blind faith and the worship of gods, and for conversion to Buddhism. Ironically, it is the main Hindu political party of Maharashtra which has recognised my efforts. I have fought against the views of the Hindu party, Shiv Sena, for many years. Their slogan is: "We're proud to be Hindu". The founder of this party, who is known as the Don of Maharashtra because of his demolishing mosques and creating communal riots, invited me to receive an award for my work. At first I refused. I had never stood on the same platform as his party. I was always fighting against them. How could I come? But my friends told me to go, because it was a move towards ending casteism. When I accepted and went to collect my award, he touched my feet in front of a huge audience and said: "I salute you for your work." I was given this award because the party respected my social work and saw that I had not done it for money. I have no big house; my work has always been for the people. I'm 74, and I'm still working for the movement, because there is a lot to be done if we are to achieve Dr. Ambedkar's dream.

Golden Jubilee
Converted 2006
I am rid of caste

I converted to Buddhism on October 2, 2006. I made the decision that I wanted to know about more about Buddhism and more about Ambedkar. I wanted to have a mind free from casteism. When I took *deeksha*, recited the five precepts and the 22 vows publicly with 92 other people, I felt at peace. My mind felt purified, as if a great weight had been lifted from my heart. Right now I feel free as a bird.

During the past six months I have been preparing for this rebirth by attending seminars about Ambedkar and Buddhism. Two hundred of us came from my community, Tamil Nadu and Pondicherry, for this event, but some of us were not prepared to take *deeksha*. Those of us who did feel ready dressed in white and walked through the huge crowds to take refuge in the Buddha, Dhamma and Sangha. I still can't believe that yesterday I had the courage to stand in front of thousands of people and let them witness me taking refuge. I feel reborn. Before, I hated crowds, and would rarely attend public events with my husband. I am a shy person, but from somewhere I found the courage to walk through all those people to the conversion place and take my rebirth.

It has been the most profound experience in my life. Standing up in front of thousands of people and showing them that I as a Dalit am converting on the same day that so many of my people converted fifty years ago, I felt connected to the past and the future. Yesterday thousands of us Dalits took *deeksha* throughout the day in different places in Nagpur. I felt connected to all of them. I know now I have to go back to my people and help spread the word about conversion.

I have this overwhelming feeling of wanting to help others in the way that Ambedkar helped many of my people in the past. Before my conversion I felt quite different. I was in conflict with my husband because he was often out of the house doing social work in the Dalit community. He works for the liberation of the Dalit people. I've been a traditional Hindu Indian woman all my life. This means that my concerns have been the family, the children and the house. I wanted my husband to have the same priorities but his work seemed to come first. Sometimes I was irritated with him, and criticised him for his work. Before the conversion my mind seemed stressed with being a housewife. I had no confidence to do anything more. I am illiterate in the sense that I am not able to read and write, while my husband is highly qualified. When he went out to do public speaking and speak to the masses, I felt jealous, even angry, because I couldn't communicate in this way. But now I have seen reality and realise all I need is compassion and I too could help my people.

I am not from the State of Maharashtra, and converting is a major concern in my community. It is new, although we've known that many of our *Mahar* Dalit brothers and sisters have converted long before this year, and that has been part of their upliftment out of casteism. The majority of Dalit castes are still stuck at the bottom of the caste system. I hate the caste system. Where I live there is still a lot of discrimination, to the extent that some high caste people fear that if they touch anything we touch they will be polluted. I know the caste system must be destroyed and in my own way I have tried to challenge it. I married a *Sudra* from the labouring caste, and his caste is higher than mine, as I am from the Scheduled Caste. I didn't care that I would upset my parents and my in-laws. I loved him, and that was what counted. I was fortunate because my husband's family treat me like one of their daughters and have been very kind to me. It was my family who put up the fight. They didn't want me to break tradition, and refused to accept my marriage. They were angry with me for several years, but have gradually come round to the idea. The Dalits in Tamil Nadu have not been exposed to as much progressive thinking as those in the State of Maharashtra and so it is a big struggle to challenge the entire Hindu culture.

I was born in Pondicherry, which was ruled by the French government until 1954, so there is more forward thinking on caste issues. But just 25 kilometres away in Tamil Nadu, where my husband works, the situation is very different. There are so many caste problems we still face. For example, the *chai* shops have one teacup for the Dalit and one teacup for the high caste Hindu. Dalits cannot sit in the shop; we must stand and drink our *chai* as quickly as possible. There are bus stops for Dalits and bus stops for caste Hindus. Some state buses refuse to let Dalits sit down; we have to stand while the high caste people take all the seats.

Many of the Dalit people in Tamil Nadu are still forced to do scavenging work. We still have to carry dead bodies and animals out of the village, and we are still expected to serve the Brahmins. Many of the Dalits are unaware that they do not have to do this work, that it isn't their destiny because of bad karma. So many of us still believe it is our duty to serve the Brahmins in the hope that in our next life we will be born into a slightly better caste. So many of us still worship the Hindu gods and go to the temples and offer devotional rituals outside the doors.

The three major Dalit groups in this area are the *Pallas*, the *Paraiyars* and the *Arunthathiyars*, who are at the bottom, and are responsible for scavenging. The situation in Tamil Nadu is very pathetic. The people do not know much about Buddhism and Ambedkar. They know that Ambedkar has done something, but they have no idea of his philosophy, though wherever you go you will see statues and pictures of him. More Dalits in Tamil Nadu have converted to Christianity and Islam than to Buddhism. There is a real fear that if we convert to Buddhism, we will become isolated. We have been taught that Lord Buddha is an incarnation of the god Vishnu, and that he is thus part of Hindu culture. The idea of Buddhism is still new in our state. Also, if people convert, who will want to marry their daughters and sons? If they leave Hinduism they believe that bad things will happen to their families. They also fear Ambedkar's ideas on education. What is the use of educating their daughters when they go and live with their husband's family? Some see the value of educating their sons because this could bring money into the family, but people still tend to think: "Why spend money on educating your children when what the family needs is food?" Even if state education is provided at low cost, many of the parents still influence their children to work and help with the family income.

This is where the work and education needs to be done. During my *deeksha,* I could see the fate of these people, and knew I must step out of my conditioning, that is, my home, and begin to educate these people away from Hinduism. I want them to be rid of caste as this is the thing that is enslaving them. It is the women I feel most concerned about, as my husband has often come home troubled about the sexual harassment women face from non-Dalit men. I found it hard to believe, and often didn't want to hear about it. But now I feel an urge to find out more and see what I can do to help. Many of these women from the castes I've just mentioned are dependent on working in the fields for the high caste Hindus. They are forced to accept low wages, and if they don't accept them, the landlords rape them, and some have even been killed.

I am hoping to get involved with some organisations which try to help these women by taking action. I couldn't believe it when my husband sat me down one day and said: "You have to listen. Many of these women complain to the police about these atrocities and often because the police are Brahmins they will not register the complaints. Since the perpetrators are Brahmins the women don't stand a chance. They need people like you to help them." So much has been flooding into my mind since the conversion just over 24 hours ago. All the things my husband has been trying to teach me are beginning to make sense. I didn't feel able to do anything. I often wondered why he was telling me. But now I see he wants me to help him in his work. I feel committed to help these women at any cost. I am in a position to do this because I was brought up in Pondicherry where the conditions for us Dalits are much better. We don't have such a big inferiority problem. Education is provided for most of us in Pondicherry, and most parents will educate their children till they are 16. All my three children have been successfully educated. One of my sons has majored in French and English, and the others are in professional careers. It is very rare for Dalit men in our state to do so well. And the children who are born today in Tamil Nadu stand little chance of being educated beyond the age of 12.

My conversion has given me a direction for my life. It's come at a time when all my sons have turned 18, so I can fully commit myself to the emancipation of the Dalits in India. My husband talks about organisation, education and agitation. I hope to do all of this for the freedom of Dalit people throughout India. I will support him in his work, but also become involved with other organisations. I especially want freedom for women and their children. I want to stop the abuses which are happening. I believe Ambedkar is more than another god; he is our saviour; he is the answer for our people.

Ambedkarites Spreading the Mission

Dalits are duty born
To work for his mission
Dr Ambedkar

I was born in 1959 and brought up in the house we're sitting in right now in the ward of Kamptee, part of the city of Nagpur, in the State of Maharashtra. My father was a Labour leader and in the years between 1972 and 1978 he was a Member of Parliament. Unfortunately, I could not work with my father because of his untimely death on October 14, 1982, exactly 26 years to the day after Dr. Ambedkar did the mass conversion. My father's family converted from 'Untouchable' to Buddhist at that time. Because I saw my father working for his community, the 'downtrodden', I saw how socially committed he was. I also saw that even though my father was educated he was still treated badly by the high caste people.

I wished to work with my father in my youth. I was brought up in the atmosphere of my father working for his Dalit community, so I felt I was born to do this work. After he died, I took up his work, which was the Ambedkar mission campaigning for the freedom of the Dalits. I was 22 years old when my father died, and I remember seeing the thousands of people at his funeral and realising then that I had no choice but to continue his work.

Shortly after the funeral, I began working for the rights

of *bidi* workers who make traditional leaf cigarette. My father struggled to get proper working conditions for these workers, 80 per cent of whom were women, and all from the Scheduled Castes. They were being treated appallingly. In India many rules and regulations are written down on paper, but when it comes to the case of the Scheduled Castes, very few of these rules actually get implemented. This is because people know they can get away with avoiding the law when it comes to the Dalit community.

The campaign came to a crunch when one day over 800 workers turned up for work and found that the owner had closed the factory down, without giving any warning or even asking permission from the government. This was an illegal act, so we went on an eight-day hunger strike, and approached the government over the next two years to give the workers some compensation. Finally, the government gave in, making other factories re-employ the workers and paying a token monetary compensation.

During this time I was elected Mayor of my ward, Kamptee, and became the youngest Mayor to be elected in the State of Maharashtra. I was elected three times from 1985. In my last term I was also elected as a member of the Legislative Assembly of Maharasntra. This was an achievement as I was elected not through the reservation policy but in the general constituency, where people from all castes and genders can stand, and there is no stipulation saying the post must go to a Dalit or a woman.

In 1999 I became the State Minister of Water. I had already had experience working with water issues, as in Kamptee we were without our own water supply for many years. It became so bad that men refused to marry girls from Kamptee because we had no fresh water. However, once I became state minister, I was able to ensure that my ward had its own independent supply.

Since 2004 I've not been in a political position but I have been taking work that helps people feel united and become involved with politics. I am an unimportant person but I have the life that I have to live, and being born a Dalit means I must continue to work for the mission. I am inspired by Ambedkar's mission. Whatever my community have, it is because of him. If he had not been born in India we would still all be 'Untouchable'. So I am influenced more by social commitment than politics. Ambedkar said that the people must be educated if they were to progress. When you travel around the state of Maharashtra you will see that there are Dalit people who are educated and have respectable jobs, and live in houses with fresh water. This is because of Ambedkar. This is because he led the people to embrace Buddhism. My father did this, along with thousands of other people. And today, fifty years later, we are celebrating the Golden Jubilee, celebrating the many changes that have happened since then. But I want to work for the people because we have not got 100 per cent of what Ambedkar wanted, and so the mission continues.

The changes we see in the city have not yet happened in the villages. Even in the State of Maharashtra, where the mass conversion took place and where the majority of the *Mahar* caste have achieved social upliftment, there are still villages where people cannot drink from a common well. The Dalits of all castes are still living on the perimeter of the villages, which identifies them as belonging to the Scheduled Castes. Many villagers still don't have access to education.

So my life is about working for the education of my people. I am fortunate not to have any brothers, because in India brothers are extremely dominating, and if their sisters aren't married they believe it is their right to arrange a marriage. This is because they believe that if their sister remains single, it will create a major problem for the family. How will their sister live, where will she stay? I made a decision to remain single so I could devote myself to the people. If I had married, I would have had to have been dutiful to my in-laws all my life. I've been living alone with my mother and my youngest sister for the past 24 years.

What I have found is that women are fighting for their rights in many countries; the confidence of women is an international problem. Of course, it's a bigger problem when the women are illiterate and poor, and that's very often the case in India. I believe that there is no difference between a boy and a girl. It is how we define ourselves that matters. If we look at ourselves as female and think that because of this we have to marry, have children, cook and clean, that will have a huge effect on us. We will underestimate ourselves and have no self-confidence.

Once my eldest sister was married, much pressure was put on me to marry, but I told my parents that if they continued to force me into this situation, I would leave home. My mother told my father: "We have given her an education; she must have the right to make her own decisions." I knew quite early that if I married, I would not be able to work for the people. I would not be able to make my own decisions; my husband would make them for me. The decision not to marry came from within me. I saw the people crying at my father's funeral, and that was it, I didn't look back.

I am not suggesting that all women in India don't get married, because in the villages this would be extremely hard, with all the cultural conditioning. I realise that it is because of my position that I can remain single, strong and confident. When I give lectures to women, I tell them to see themselves not as ladies, but as human beings, and to realise that they have everything that a human being requires. I encourage them to motivate themselves and go on their independent way. I never think: "I'm a woman." I just work as a human being. This is part of Ambedkar's mission, educating people, and that includes women. I work out of my sense of duty to the mission, and this is very satisfying. I don't claim to be the only person doing this, of course; Ambedkar's mission is so huge that all of us are workers.

I work on three levels simultaneously. First, I work in the social field, helping people if they have experienced injustices in employment, from the police or the criminal justice system, supporting women if they have been sexually abused or raped. Secondly, I try to work on an economic and cultural level. During the time of the *bidi* workers' hunger strike, I made friends with a Japanese upasika Buddhist woman. She had come to visit India to see what I was doing. She was shocked to see that we were all on hunger strike to try to get our rights. After she returned to Japan she offered financial support to the *bidi* workers, but she also wanted to offer a cultural hall for the children. So together we constructed the Dragon Palace in Nagpur, which has become an international monument. This palace, with the Lord Buddha's statue erected on the first floor, has become a cultural centre for all the people of Nagpur. It is open to people of all castes and status, and even the poor labourer feels at home here. Everyone can feel the friendship, peace and harmony. The Buddha's thought should not be restricted to one community. This was not Ambedkar's idea; he wanted the whole of India to convert. I also believe that everyone who wants happiness, contentment and stillness in their lives should adopt Buddhism.

The third level is the political field. Actually I'm not political or ambitious, but I know that if I want to do my social work and fulfil my commitment to the community, I must have a political weapon. So I have set up a political party, the Bahujan

Republic Ekta Munch Party. This is because many people working for the mission are scattered, so I am trying my best to bring all of us together. If I don't have a political banner, a united front, people will not take me seriously. I am aware that political parties just want to know what castes and how many castes are in their constituency so they can plan their campaign accordingly. My political party is not concerned with this. It is for the social emancipation of the Dalit community.

In fact, my direction for the next ten to fifteen years is towards religious work, because I have seen that this is what makes people truly happy. I have observed an organisation called the TBMSG which has allowed lay people to practise Buddhism. They include children and teach families about Ambedkar. Before this group came to this country, we only had monks preaching Buddhism. There was no place for lay people, just the practice of lay people offering alms and *dana* to the monks.

Although I don't see the need to align myself with a specific Buddhist *sangha*, I can see that India needs more groups like TBMSG to help us, groups which are spiritually motivated and focussed while also spreading the word of Ambedkar. In the State of Maharashtra there is no village where there are no Buddhists. At a minimum you will find that at least 5 per cent of the population has converted. But if you speak to the 'Buddhists', you find that they know very little about the religion, or are mixing Hinduism and Buddhism together.

The media has done nothing to help the situation. While we were celebrating fifty years of the conversion, the Hindus were celebrating many gods and *devas*, and not one piece of electronic news covered Ambedkar's anniversary; they just covered the Hindu festivals. We have to use the media if we want to encourage the knowledge of Buddhism. People come home and turn the television on to only Hindu culture.

Caste cannot be eradicated because the main base of the media and politics in India is caste. When people meet me, they are not interested in me. They are only interested in my caste. I, the human being, comes second. Yes, you can say that Buddhism is helping to abolish caste to some extent. We Buddhists have become more powerful. But at this 2006 *deeksha* in Nagpur, only 25 per cent of the people who came to celebrate the anniversary were educated. The other 75 per cent had no shoes, no good clothes on their backs, and carried their food on their heads. Many walked for days because they couldn't afford trains or bus tickets. This picture has to be changed if our people are to become economically strong.

We have to change the situation in the villages, in the slums and the cities. I am currently demanding that every house in the slums be improved, to have its own private toilet and bathroom. I also want every house to be regularised when they are developed. By this I mean that all the houses should have the names of both men and women on the outside. I believe that when a woman marries a man she should have equal rights. If they are married, they both own their house. Ambedkar was asking for this 55 years ago in his Hindu Code Bill, which is still pending.

Education has become very costly right now. There is a great deal of privatisation happening in the country; all the government institutions are becoming privatised, including the schools and colleges. Although the provision of government education is still available, many Dalit students will not have access to better education because all the resources are being invested in private education. People who want to study have to pay many thousands of rupees. This will make it impossible for my people to take higher education and have the opportunity to become a doctor or enter into a profession, so I am demanding that the private institutions should have to set aside reserved places, because it is not possible for my community to pay the fees they ask for.

Also, many industries are coming to India and privatising government institutions like telecommunications. These private companies don't have any reservation policies, so now Dalits find it harder to get work. So I am pushing for reservations in the private sector. We have to move very fast. This Congress government promised that they would introduce a new reservation policy for the people, but they have forgotten, so I am doing my duty and reminding them of Ambedkar's mission.

I'm a product of
Ambedkar's philosophy
Educate Dalits

I work for the education of my community. Twenty-seven years ago I was born into the Scheduled Caste. My family was very poor, like most Dalit families. My father drove a cycle rickshaw and my mother sold anything she could to help make things meet. When I was about five, my father managed to get a job as a cleaner on the railways, but there still wasn't enough money for five children, so he worked during the day cleaning and then late into the night on his rickshaw.

I was the talented one of the family and so my education was supported. I went to a school with students from all castes, but I never faced any prejudice because the high caste people respected my intelligence. I went to a Trust school, which was different from a government school. Up to the mid-1990s high caste teachers in government schools were not very good, because their jobs were secure and they knew they could get away with casteism.

Since I managed to get a high percentage in my exams when I was 11, I was given a place in a Trust school and my parents didn't have to pay any fees. My father was a staunch Ambedkarite and so he believed in education for his entire family. Although my parents are illiterate, they still encouraged culture and the arts. My father was a singer and poet, and my mother loved to tell us stories. From my youth I was immersed in the philosophies of Dr. Ambedkar, and made a decision at 11 that I would become a teacher so I could help educate the society. My father said that this was the most important thing to do.

I have been teaching for 7 years; I began aged 21. I work at a government school, because this is where the children need me. Private schools attract most of the best teachers, but I wanted to work within my community. In my school the government gives a full grant to each student, so parents do not have the excuse that they can't pay fees. The school's population is 100 per cent Dalit, because it is located in an all-Dalit area. The school was founded in 1964, and many prominent Dalits have been educated there. It was the inspiration of Dr. Panjabrao Deshmukh, who worked with Dr. Ambedkar. He was also born into a Dalit family, but became highly educated and had an intercaste marriage. Inspired by Ambedkarism he opened up a trust for Dalit people, so that he could run many schools and colleges in Dalit villages.

Educating Dalit children from the villages is different from teaching those who grow up in well-served cities where they have all the basic facilities they need. I work with five to ten year olds, and when they arrive aged five, the first thing we have to do is to teach them how to sit and eat. Their parents are out at work from 4 or 5 in the morning and there has been no one to teach them basic manners and etiquette.

Although there are no high caste children in my school we still have casteism. Caste is endemic in Indian culture. Parents tell their children which caste they are in and teach them about the hierarchy. Parents who are OBC tell their kids that they are higher than the common Scheduled Castes, and much fighting among the different castes happens in the playground and in class. Another problem we face in the Dalit community is that many parents are just not interested in educating their children, despite the fact the government will offer a grant for their fees. They would rather their children were out working and helping them to sell flowers, or scavenging for paper to sell to factories for recycling, or working in the fields. Because of the government rule they have to send their children to school up to the age of 12, but after that, many marry off their daughters or put the boys out to work. And there are still large percentages that don't send their children beyond the age of ten, or even eight. So educating my community is a challenge. I feel personally hurt when children leave school at such an early age. I feel I have failed them, failed the Ambedkar mission, especially if they are very talented. It's a waste of their life when they have to go and help their parents sell on the streets. Many of these children are frustrated. You can see this because many of the clever ones who leave become drug addicts. They don't give all the money they make to their parents; they keep some for themselves and begin buying, an addictive tobacco which you chew. Many of these children end up having mouth cancer and terrible health problems, especially in the digestive area.

Interestingly, it is the girls who are becoming better educated. They seem to stay on at school till 12, but after this they are often married because of economic problems. The parents believe that if their daughter gets married early it will give her all the security she needs, and they will not have to worry about her any more. After she has completed her education up to 12, as soon as there is someone available, she will be married. If these girls were encouraged to stay on at school many of them would end up with good careers. But convincing their parents of this is almost impossible.

Part of my work as a teacher takes place outside the school, in the village where the children live. I go from door to door and try to communicate with the parents. When some parents complain that the government grant is not enough for their children's books and uniforms, I will offer to help support their child if I think he or she has potential. I am happy to spend my own money to support a child's education and prevent the parents using the excuse of not having enough money. I try to help parents break a traditional habit of thinking. They think that education can't benefit their children. They don't understand how it will help their families. They don't understand the value of education. My mission is to continue to be of service as a teacher. If I am able to help one student a year to continue with their education I am satisfied. I will do my best to help all my students because I believe education is the gateway to freedom. If Dalit children are educated, their status will change. If they remain illiterate, society will cheat them. Education may not guarantee them a job, but it will at least give them skills to cope with day-to-day life, and they will be treated more positively. The reason why I have so much confidence is because of my success in studies, and because I know that Ambedkarism works for my community.

Ambedkar hated
Snake in the Hindus' garden
Praised by Dalits

I remember that Dr. Ambedkar once said he was the most hated person in India because of his caste, but he still got himself very well educated. When I visit his memorial *vihara* in Mumbai, I see how much he is respected because people come from all over to pay their tributes to him and pay obeisance to his picture. He was hated by many upper caste Hindus and once wrote: "I am like a snake in the Hindu garden." He is still hated by some because they don't appreciate his contribution to Indian society. Whenever I talk to Brahmins or other high caste people they always say that he didn't do much great work because he only worked for the *Mahar* community. They only mention his negative aspects. They remind me that he was harsh and rude to people. I can see that casteism is so strong and subtle that they look at him through the spectacles of caste. Even Brahmins who have converted to Buddhism still have strong conditioning and do not see him in a good light. I tell them that I don't criticise a Brahmin if they have done good work, so why do they criticise Ambedkar?

I believe we must see beyond caste. Often people say they don't believe in caste, caste is imagination, but when it comes to giving credit to certain people they still have casteism in their thinking. I feel there has been an injustice to Ambedkar, because he did extraordinary work for the whole of India. He is the author of the Constitution of India, the father of the Indian Republic. His work has benefited the whole of India, not just the *Mahar* community.

People need to read his writings properly. He didn't just campaign for the *Mahars*. Yes, he was a *Mahar*, and his people followed him in conversion. This is part of our caste conditioning: you follow the leader of your caste. But Ambedkar wanted all downtrodden people to come together. He wanted the Scheduled Caste people, other Backward Caste people, and Scheduled Tribes to come together and unite, because they would then become the majority in this country. His mission was for us to unite so we could be one force fighting for our human rights. He knew that if we stayed isolated in our castes, we would remain a minority, and not have much effect on the fabric of Indian cultural conditioning.

I'm an Ambedkarite because of the principles he lived his life by and fought for throughout his life: he turned his life into a religious, moral and ethical quest. He was an excellent politician, scholar and social activist, with an ethical mind. He saw that law was not enough to create an ethical country. He realised that it was religion that could change the whole thinking of a nation. And he clarified that Buddhism is the only religion that states that the human mind and the human being is the most important thing, not our caste or our birth. Because he has taught us about the great ideal of Buddha, I am an Ambedkarite.

I have a great respect for him; he is as an idol for me. I respect and salute his courage because he showed determination when there was nobody with him. When he first began his fight for the human rights of the Dalit, he was on his own and faced much prejudice. He was given no respect or recognition as a human being. He stood in front of society and said: "I am a human being like you. I have a mind; I feel pain when you treat me like this. I need food, I need shelter. You are supposed to treat me like a human being."

This was never said so strongly before. Ambedkar was incredibly courageous. He was also kind-hearted, and well educated. He could have earned so much money for his own luxury, but he thought only about people who were downtrodden, people who were in need of help, and how he could uplift their lives. He once said: "I don't want you to keep praising me; I don't want you to say 'Jai Bhim!' I want you to continue my work. That is the best way of honouring me." When I read these words at college, I asked myself what I was doing for the people as a follower of Ambedkar. I was inspired by his honesty; he was straightforward, outspoken and transparent. He spoke out against Mahatma Gandhi, the one who was made into the biggest hero of that era, credited for being the campaigner for the 'Untouchables'. Other people never dared to challenge Gandhi but he did, arguing that

Gandhi did not want to get rid of caste in India. All Gandhi did was change the name of the 'Untouchables'. He did nothing about getting rid of the four *varnas*. Ambedkar tried to get rid of the whole *varna* system because it was unjust.

Ambedkarism is part of my conditioning. I was born into a family which was a so-called converted new Buddhist family. My family engaged with social activities, and since my birth in 1971 I have been told about Ambedkar's ideals. My parents said: "He is the man who gave us life, the man who shaped our lives." My grandfather used to cry when he told me stories of how when he was small they never had food to eat or clothes to wear, and survived on the food that was thrown onto the floor. I watched my granny go out to meetings and host meetings in my house, and I used to listen in on these meetings, and this had an effect on my mind. I was speaking, living and breathing Ambedkar's philosophies from my youth.

I am highly educated because of his views. All I could think was: "I need to be educated." So I continued with my studies right through to graduating with a doctorate. I didn't think about what job I wanted, I was just motivated by education. When I entered the academy, I really believed that casteism was coming to an end because I received no discrimination at all. Although I grew up with extreme poverty, the only discrimination I knew about was through the stories my family told me about their lives and Dr. Ambedkar. I grew up believing that Ambedkar had made everything all right for my community, which is why I could be educated to such a high standard. We were all one during my doctorate in philosophy and when I went on to train in medical science and pathology, my experience was harmonious. When people used to say caste still existed, I just thought they were exaggerating. But when I began working in my field, I had a huge surprise. People wanted to know what caste I was, and assumed I got my job on the basis of reservations. But I have been appointed always on my own merits.

My first job was in the government hospital of Mumbai, and two of us were appointed out of seven hundred people to do research and scientific work. We were both offered training as part of our job. But after the first six months I noticed that the other woman was being sent off to all the courses. I thought that perhaps after she was trained, I would be next. I didn't think for one moment it was because she was Brahmin. After a year I hadn't been on one course. A colleague of mine returned after a sabbatical year, and he took me aside and said: "Have you told people here you are Buddhist?" I said: "Yes." He said: "You have made a big mistake. Have you experienced any discrimination?" I realised in that moment that I had been doing much of the labouring work and hardly any of the scientific work I had been employed for. When I realised this, I resigned.

I was then appointed, again on the merit of my professional ability, to head a small department in another government hospital. The people I worked with were resistant from the start. They were not interested in my suggestion of team work; in fact they tried to make false allegations against me, complaining about me and watching for every mistake I made. I was informed that they were resentful because a Dalit had been employed as their boss on a permanent basis, while most of them were on temporary contracts. This kind of discrimination is common for us Dalits when we are educated and are in positions of responsibility and power. We are harassed so much that many of us resign. You have to be tough and strong to survive. My experiences at work have opened my eyes. I have seen a different face of the world now. Even the Dalit people I worked with wouldn't cooperate because they were not used to one of their own or a woman being in charge.

All this made me see that Ambedkar's vision has not been completely realised.

Being an Ambedkarite who just agitates is not enough to challenge these issues. It's not enough to shout about how bad the Hindus are and become violent. Education is important because with it you can enter the mainstream of society, but it is still not enough. We must be ethical too if we are to work for the welfare of all beings. Ambedkar said: "I'm not holding a sword; my pen is my sword." His was a battle of paper. He was so educated that he was able to change many constitutional rules as a politician. And because of his ethics he was able to change the world of many Dalits in India. His legacy lives through every single one of us who are educated, with professional jobs and positions of power. We are the result of his great compassionate work. How can we not be Ambedkarites? How can we not work for his mission?

Young Voices

Young teenage voices
Naïve, bold and innocent
Words of the future

Dr. Ambedkar was a highly educated man from the Dalit community. He had to struggle. He was tortured in his childhood, and experienced a lot of 'Untouchability' and discrimination problems. Casteism is a great problem in India because the Brahmins are the high society of India and they believe we Dalits are inferior. I know this because I go to an English school where many of the children are from different backgrounds, and I have often experienced discrimination. I am fourteen and have already had to begin fighting prejudice battles. The teachers make the high caste girls do all the public functions; they prefer the upper castes to represent the school whenever we have festivals and major events.

When I was ten, some of the children came to know that my father is Buddhist, and so they stopped talking to me and involving me in their games. I was often left out. I told my teacher and she was kind and told the girls to include me again. I know as a Dalit I must work hard, or I will not gain success in what I want to do. I want to be a software engineer when I grow up.

Even though I am laughed at sometimes for being a Buddhist, I am proud of my parents because they work for other people and they care about the community. Although my mother does so much hard work outside the house, she still manages to care for me and my younger brother.

I'm sixteen and was born in Amravati in May 1991. I grew up with Dalits, and I went to a school with them. It was an Ambedkar school, and we were taught about Ambedkar and learned to meditate as well as learning how to read and write. For me, Buddha Siddhartha and Dr. Ambedkar mean immense freedom. I learned in school how he suffered for my people and about his pain. Because of his struggle, my generation are at the next stage. We've had the privilege of education.

My parents' generation weren't as independent as my generation. They had to work for others. But my friends and I can work for ourselves and set up our own businesses. I've just left school at sixteen and now I do sewing work for ladies. I enjoy this work very much, because it's been my hobby since childhood.

I'm 17 and I don't want to get married because I want to fulfil my dreams. If I get married, I will have to do what my in-laws want me to do. That will mean cooking and cleaning for them. My parents are beginning to pressurise me because I've just failed some exams. They have warned me if I fail again, I will have to marry. So I am trying my hardest to pass the exam next time. I know if I can continue in my studies this will delay my marriage, and if I am lucky it may lead to a job.

I think it is dangerous for women to marry before they are eighteen, and dangerous for their children too because at that age we don't know much at all about marriage and we are not prepared for it. I know Babasaheb's wish was for the Dalits to educate themselves. He was a great man; because of him more Dalit women and girls are becoming independent. This is an achievement for my people.

I was born in a small village outside Amravati 18 years ago. I have two brothers and three sisters. My father sells vegetables and fruit on the streets, and my mother is a housewife.

I went to a government school and I enjoyed it very much because the teachers gave us good books and made us work hard. We learned about Dr. Ambedkar and I'm grateful for the facilities he provided for my community by writing the Indian constitution. My parents believe in both Dr. Ambedkar and the Buddha. They brought me up on stories about the Buddha and told me he was the god of compassion.

I'm not interested in working for other people because I know my parents' generation have suffered working for the Brahmins. I want to create my own job. I would like to give coaching to children whose parents can't afford to send them to school. My advice to Dalit girls is that life isn't just about education. We have to have our basic equal rights

---

I was born in Badnera in 1991. My father died shortly after I was born, so I am the youngest of seven children. My mother is a labourer in the construction business and works very hard to bring all of us up properly. I try to help my mother in the home, but there isn't much to do because my older sister does most things. I left school at 14 because my mother did not have enough money to support me, so now I help one of my older sisters with her children.

I have seen how hard it is for women to bring up children on their own. My mother mixes cement and carries it on her head in a pot, and gives it to the men so they can build the roads. She suffers from great pain in her knees and shoulders and sometimes goes to bed crying. I don't want to do the work that my mother does, but I'm not sure what I can do without much education. Fortunately, my mother is not asking me to marry, so I have some time to try and create a business for myself. Ideally I would like to return to my studies, so I can educate myself properly and get a proper job.

Discovering Trailokya Bauddha Mahasangha, Sahayak Gana

Follows the dhamma
At any cost to her life
Heroic husband

I am 58, almost 59. I was born in 1949 in a small village in the locality of Khatav. Like all Dalits we lived on the perimeter of the village. I was born an 'Untouchable' and grew up in a Hindu household for the first seven years of my life. We practised many Hindu rituals. I remember my parents fasting a lot and praying to many gods and goddesses and visiting many temples. We could only worship the gods by standing outside, though; we weren't allowed in. I also remember people giving my family broken cups to drink out of whenever we visited a chai shop, and how people would offer us our drinks with their arms outstretched as if they would drop down dead if we accidentally touched them. I went to a school with all the village children, so we 'Untouchables' were in the same class as Brahmins and other high caste Hindus. Whenever I visited my friends from the Brahmin caste, their parents would treat me differently. They gave me stale and bad food to eat, while their daughters had very fresh food to eat. But I was young and didn't really understand why people were like this to me and other 'Untouchables'.

When I was seven, in 1956, my father converted to Buddhism. He went to Nagpur and took *deeksha* from Dr. Ambedkar, and he was so inspired when he came back that he marched about the house and pulled down every picture of gods and goddesses we had and drowned them in the well. He suggested my mother took conversion too, and proposed that we visit the nearby town where there were many celebrations happening relating to Dr. Ambedkar. Many of my friends' parents were doing the same. In fact, most of us 'Untouchables', who lived on the perimeter of my village, converted. There were celebrations every day for two weeks.

Some of the Brahmins seemed to be really angry with my community; they refused to serve us in shops for a while. This discrimination happened for many years. When we celebrated the date of Babasaheb's conversion and his birthday, a fight would often break out. The Brahmins despised our having processions and festivals to commemorate these prestigious dates, and often they would beat up some of the Buddhist men very badly. But our people never retaliated. They didn't believe in violence, because Babasaheb had insisted that our emancipation should be non-violent.

I remember the day he died. I had completed my seventh year. I came home from school and found that my father had disappeared to Mumbai and my mother was crying hysterically, "Babasaheb is no more." She was even banging her head against the wall and wailing. I thought this was strange, and asked her: "Why are you crying about a stranger? You didn't even know him or meet him." My mother exploded; she was furious with me and beat me. From that moment I wanted to know who this man was. I felt compelled to find out about him and his work.

Although my parents were illiterate, they understood the value of education. They wanted all three of their children to be able to read and write and have some education. The village school only went up to the age of 11, so my father took me to Mumbai where my older brother lived with his wife. The plan was that I would further my education with the support of my brother and his new family. But as soon as my father left me there, my brother's wife began to treat me with no respect. She would laugh at me and say: "You're just a poor village girl." I suffered a lot because she and my brother began to treat me badly. My brother seemed to forget about his roots. He was earning good wages but didn't want to pay a nominal fee towards my education. I reminded him of how hard our parents had worked for us, how they had slaved away working in the fields and building roads, but he just laughed and didn't seem to care. He refused to give me any money, and stopped sending money home to my parents, so I challenged him, and this made my life in their house worse.

After a couple of years of struggling in this household, I decided that I wasn't going to live with my brother and his wife any more, and that the only way out was to get married. I told them I wanted to marry, and my sister-in-law began talking about inappropriate men. I could tell they were bad. They stank of alcohol and tobacco and didn't have much respect for her. So I made my own choice about whom to marry. There was a young man across the road from where my brother lived who seemed to like me. He had shown some interest and seemed quite suitable, so I agreed to marry him. I didn't want my sister-in-law to choose a man for me. They called my father and he came from the village. He asked this man's father if he would agree to provide education for me, and my father-in-law agreed, so my father was happy. I married at 16, and my father-in-law kept his promise and sent me to college, but my sister-in-law began to complain because there was nobody to do the housework.

We lived with my husband's elder sister and her husband and his brother and wife in one small room in Mumbai. My husband was the youngest in the family so had to do whatever he was told. With so little space in our home, tension mounted. My husband wasn't earning much money and I saw myself as the problem, as I was the only one who wasn't contributing to the home, so I left college. I became pregnant quite soon after that. Unfortunately my husband had typhoid and became quite sick during my pregnancy. Since he was the youngest, he had to sleep outside on the roof as there was not enough space for all of us, but because he was ill he couldn't sleep outside any more, so I agreed to sit in a small corner all night while he slept. I was eight months pregnant at the time, and sitting up all night in a crouched position was very bad for me. I miscarried and at that late stage the baby was born dead. We buried it nearby and I was taken to hospital. But somebody informed the police, and they came to investigate our household, and when they saw the living conditions they said I had to move back to my brother's house where there would be more space.

This was a difficult time, but my father-in-law continued to treat me well. He respected that I was a practising Buddhist and would take me to a *vihara* every Sunday to help me meditate and recover. My brother was sceptical. His new family were Buddhist in name only, and still insisted on doing Hindu *puja*, which wasn't helpful for me at all. He had forgotten all about our family conversion, and thought I needed to pray to the gods for help. I couldn't continue to live here either, and with my father-in-law's help we left my brother's house.

My husband rented a small room, and friends gave us utensils and basic things for the house. Our financial condition was really bad, so I had to go out and work as well. But soon we had more luck and my uncle gave us Rs. 500, and so we were able to buy a hut in one of the main slums of Mumbai. There was so much poverty where we lived and there were no proper toilets. I can still remember the days when all of us women used to go out in the roads and put up an umbrella, squat and go to the toilet. We had no choice; there was nowhere else to go. The water was filthy and during the monsoon times, water, snakes and debris would flood our homes. The dry seasons were no better: the heat was unbearable, as there were no fans in the home. Children were always falling into the sewage while playing.

I began to campaign for the rights of our slums and became quite famous. People used to knock on my door at all hours, even at 3 a.m. in the morning. I was like the social worker for the people of the slums, listening to people's problems. My home became a bit of a political office. I had a way of speaking to the political people. I managed to convince them that we needed some public toilets and clean water, otherwise people would continue to die of all sorts of diseases. I set up sewing classes for women so they could begin to earn some money and have some independence from their husbands. The daughter of the Prime Minister Nehru, Indira Gandhi, came to visit our slums during my campaign. I met her and gave her flowers; this was an auspicious event in my life. I felt very happy that I could serve poor people like myself, and wanted to use my skills even more.

Very slowly my husband and I built our lives back up again and recovered from the loss of our first child. My husband worked for a private electronic company, and I worked at home, putting together plugs and sockets with tiny screws. I also did some screen printing on saris and sold them at the market. My husband wanted me to conceive again but it didn't happen. I didn't have the same wish because I knew that children would not fulfil my needs, and so I began searching for Buddhism. I wanted to find somewhere where I could begin to follow the precepts properly and continue to help my people. This is the point where my life began.

I came across a Buddhist organisation that produced festivals and provided weddings. I became the administrator and soon I was one of the main people in this company and began to feel happy about spreading Buddhism. Many of the people I lived with were born Buddhist but didn't know what Buddhism was. I wanted my community to learn more about their Buddhist culture, and I wanted to learn more too. During the early 1970s, I began to invite a *bhikkhu* to the slums to give talks about Buddhism in return for food, clothes and donations. During the same time I came across a famous *bhikkhu* called Rahul Bodhi. He gave three hour retreats in which he taught the *vipassana* and *metta* meditations. This was all new to me and I realised there was much to learn about Buddhism.

Finally I became pregnant, and I gave birth to three children in the mid 70s, so there was a conflict between my political and social work and my children. Getting involved with spiritual practice was a big conflict too. In 1981 I attended a Rahul Bodhi three-hour retreat and when I left there was a man handing out leaflets about a Buddhist sangha called TBMSG. This pamphlet mentioned weekly classes and lectures in my locality, New Mumbai. I was curious; my parents had always told me when I was young that if I ever got the opportunity to learn more about Buddhism I must seize it. I was also curious about the four-day retreats the leaflets mentioned, and knew I must at least attend one of these. But how was I going to do this with three small children? An older friend convinced my husband that it would be a good thing for me to do and he gave me permission, agreeing to take time off work to look after our children. It was Diwali time, so there would be a great deal he could do with the children.

I never looked back. I was so happy to attend this retreat. I heard serious talks about the Dhamma, and realised that this was the thing I had been searching for in my life. It was the first time I had been around other people who called themselves Buddhist and took study seriously. I couldn't believe how we as women were treated equally, how we could all sit down and eat together. In Indian culture it is tradition for the women to feed the men first and then, after they have eaten, sit and eat in the kitchen. Here we all sat together, and the men did as much domestic work as the women. There was harmony and unity among us all, and so much positive energy too. I couldn't believe all of this.

When I returned home, I told my husband about my experience. He could see the inspiration glowing from me. He said: "It's time for you to give up your political life, your social work life, and focus on your spiritual life. I can see that the spiritual life is the place where you can grow." This was so important for me to hear. He gave me permission to work for the *Dhamma*. He supported me wholeheartedly. He was prepared to support the children and allowed me to work for the TBMSG *sangha*. He advised me to stop going on retreats led by Rahul Bodhi, and allowed me to attend retreats of three or four days while he looked after the children.

On these retreats I began to meet many different people. One person I was inspired by was a *Dhammacarini* from England called, Padmasuri. I was so inspired by her lectures. I couldn't believe that a foreigner could know more about Buddhism and Dr. Ambedkar than the people I grew up with and lived among. I told her I wanted to become like her. She encouraged me, but said that first I had to commit myself to becoming more involved with Buddhism. Then in the future, when I was ready, I could have a *Dhammacarini* Sudras, taking on the ten precepts and committing my life to the path of the Buddha, placing the Buddha, the *Dhamma* and the spiritual community at the centre of my life. She began coming to India to do retreats for women and I made sure I attended every one.

My husband continued to support me, and often took unpaid leave so I could attend all the retreats. But soon my family put pressure on him. They would laugh at him and question him, asking him why he was doing all the housework and looking after the children.

After the retreats, when I was full of inspiration, I would visit my brother and my in-laws and talk about the *Dhamma* with such enthusiasm that they too began to get excited about the Buddha, and so began to support my husband in supporting me. In 1984 my family finally moved from the slums, when we were rehoused by my husband's company. This same year I got to meet the man who was responsible for TBMSG's existence in India. That was Bhante, Urgyen Sangharakshita, the founder of the Friends of the Western Buddhist Order in England. I told Bhante that he was a great man, and that he had done great work, and that I was grateful for all the things he had done for my people. Through TBMSG I could now understand the true meaning of Dr. Ambedkar and his important work. I told him I wanted to live the life of the *sangha*. I see Bhante as being like a Buddha on earth. Because of him I can go and talk to my people and tell them why they are Buddhists, what it means to be Buddhist, and why Dr. Ambedkar advised that every Dalit should become Buddhist.

Soon after this auspicious meeting my husband began to put pressure on me. He couldn't cope with all his friends' teasing. Some people laughed at him and said: "You're the wife and she's the husband in your home." One day when I returned home from a meeting, he said: "I'm fed up. I'm not going to do the housework as well as the office work any more. You can't keep going out and leaving me with the children. I won't give you any more money." I said: "If you stop me following the *Dhamma* I will leave you and the children." We had a huge quarrel that evening.

The next day we all travelled up to his older brother's family and he said: "What can I do? She's threatening to leave me and the children because of the Buddha." I couldn't believe my ears. His brother turned to him and said: "Your wife is doing good work for our community. She's not asking you for gold or a big house. Support her to do this important work of teaching the women about Buddhism and Ambedkar in our community." Since my husband was the youngest he was always humble and obedient. After this I had no more trouble. Many husbands who didn't let their wives go on retreats were frightened of me. I was stigmatised. I was the wife who didn't perform her marital duties, and often women would refuse to speak to me, as they looked down on me for this. But I didn't care.

I became a *Dhammacarini* in 1987. I was the first, along with one other woman, Jnanasuri, to become a *Dhammacarini* in India. On the day of my Sudras, when I took *deeksha*, I could see so clearly that as humans we are all one race. I had come out of a culture that says we are all of different castes and therefore we should be treated differently. I knew that from this moment I was in the company of people who would treat every human being equally, no matter who they were. I felt so much faith and knew I was lucky to have found the true *Dhamma*.

Since my Sudras, I have been active in trying to educate women in slums and in villages about Buddhism and Dr. Ambedkar. I even left my husband in Mumbai for seven years so I could go and live in a hostel and support the young women in the community. I took my children with me too. This was difficult for my husband as he missed the children terribly. But it was important for me to help liberate my community and spread the *Dhamma*. I would like the whole world to be Buddhist. I think this was Dr. Ambedkar's vision. He didn't just want the Dalits to convert; he wanted the whole of India to convert so we could all be liberated from casteism.

I have freed myself
From the gods and goddesses
Buddha is for me

I was born a Hindu. I am from the 'ex-Untouchable' class. I am Dalit. I have been downtrodden. I am 65 and found Buddhism almost 20 years ago. I lived in a village with Marathas and Brahmins. My family worked for the Marathas. We were poor and worked in their fields. When they felt like it, they threw our food at us, and they rarely paid us. They didn't speak to us, they just shouted at us. Most of the time my family slept with our stomachs empty, and we had no proper clothes to wear. We tied things around us to try and protect ourselves from the harsh sun.

I was promised to my aunty's son before I was born. I am the eldest, and when my mother was pregnant, my aunty placed a *bindi* on my mother's stomach and said: "If this child is a girl, she will marry my son." When I was born, one of my uncles was furious I was a girl, because this meant more poverty for the family, and he tried to convince my father to bury me in the mud. But my aunt's wish saved me; she wanted me to marry her son, who was very black and ugly. When I was seven my uncle said to my father: "She has to grow up quickly so we can marry her. There is no food in this village. Let me take her to Mumbai where there is food for her to eat."

I left my family soon after this, and I was married to my cousin at 13. I was scared of my husband because he was much older than me. I never wanted him to come home because I was frightened that he might touch me. I was not happy in his home. But then my first child was born. I relaxed and gave birth to five more children. There wasn't enough money in the home, so I went to people's houses and washed their pots and pans. After every birth I was back at work in 20 days. My husband didn't have a good character. He drank too much, and beat me daily. But my mother-in-law was kind and tried to stop him if she caught him beating me.

My mother-in-law encouraged me to worship the gods so I could end my suffering and my poverty. I worshipped Khandabo. I had given birth to three girls and no boy, so I prayed to him to give me a boy. My mother-in-law and I chopped the head off a goat and offered its blood to the gods and begged that my next child would be a boy. Our prayers were answered; my fourth child was a boy. But although I also prayed to Khandabo to end my poverty, I remained poor.

When my mother-in-law died, I began to wonder about the gods I worshipped. I wondered why I was still poor after many years of worship. I said to myself: "I've been doing this god thing for so long and I'm still poor. My husband still beats me." I felt so desperate when she died that I tried to kill myself. I poured kerosene all over my clothes and said to my husband: "Here, take this matchbox and burn me." He ran from me and called a friend to rescue me. She gave me a bath.

I began searching for something after this, and I was fortunate that I had a neighbour who was involved with a Buddhist sangha called TBMSG. He introduced me to Buddhism. He said: "You have had so much suffering in your life. Maybe if you come to a retreat it will help you." I wasn't interested to begin with. I was too frightened that the gods might punish me and create more suffering in my life. A few months later two Buddhist women from TBMSG came to conduct a funeral in the slum I was living in. I felt moved by the whole programme. I felt something inside me stirring, and I wanted to communicate with the two women. They invited me to come on a retreat. I found the courage and decided to go. I thought: "My life can't get any worse, with or without the gods." It was the retreat when the first two Indian women were ordained. I felt inspired that two women could have such an important position in the religious *Sangha*. I had never seen a woman with status in my community before.

I made friends at the retreat quickly and invited them to my house, and my husband was very impressed with their warmth and kindness. He said: "Not even our own relatives are as kind as this. I am so pleased you want to be part of their *sangha*." I couldn't believe it, but after their second visit, he went around the house destroying and throwing out all our Hindu gods. I felt very scared. What was I going to do without my gods if things became worse? And what about my neighbours, what would they say? My husband ignored my laments, and even took water, bowed down to me and washed my feet. He changed radically. He stopped beating me, and if we had a strong clash, I could call my *sangha* friends who would speak to him. He developed a strong trust in them. He was impressed because they didn't demand money from him like all our relatives did, and when he was sick they were the first to visit, while our relatives took time to come.

I realised that if I wanted to get rid of my poverty I had to stop worshipping the gods. I saw that praying to the gods was blind faith and just made me poorer. I took out loans to try and do the work of the gods. I realised I had to use my energy and work hard. If I wanted to be able to buy more than one sari a year, I had to focus on the real issue. What could I do to change my life? I began with the *maitri bhavana*, the meditation of loving kindness that the TBMSG people taught me. I began to think positively about my husband, and direct positive thoughts to him, and towards my son, who was always fighting. I stopped blaming the gods for my unhappiness and poverty. I began to like myself and even believe in myself. I had no confidence before and hated everything about myself.

I even decided to go out and see if I could find some domestic work. I'm the only one with work in my large family, and I feel proud that I can feed all my grandchildren and their parents. No god has done this for me. It's through all my efforts to try to do something for myself and my family. The TBMSG retreats have taught me this.

My family-in-law still try to encourage me to worship the gods to end my poverty. Every time something goes wrong in my life they tell me it's because I have stopped praying to the gods. I tell them to leave me alone. I listen with one ear and not with the other. I don't feel angry or irritated any more. I try not to react and be cross with them. The practice of *maitri* has taught me happiness.

Two years ago, when my husband was dying of mouth cancer, he requested that a Buddhist person should come to help him die. A man came from the TBMSG to see him, and a few hours after he left, my husband died. I am so happy he died with peace in his heart because he believed in Buddhism. Although he gave me trouble in my life, I can forgive him.

I am hoping to have a *Dhammacarini* Sudras, so I can continue to develop myself within TBMSG. I have no education but I am drawn to studying the *Dhamma*. I feel loving kindness towards everyone. I am rid of the gods and goddesses. I am no longer a passive and dependent Indian housewife.

Once Buddhist in name
Ignorant was I till
TBMSG

I grew up in one of the oldest slums in Maharashtra. My grandparents were part of the mass conversion of *Mahars* to Buddhism. Before that we were known as 'Untouchables'.

Although my father's parents converted, they still held on to some Hindu and Muslim traditions. My grandmother worked in a Muslim temple to earn money, and my grandfather worked for the high caste Hindus in the fields, so they were still treated as 'Untouchable'. And my grandparents themselves were affected by the *Manusmriti*, the Hindu text that all low caste people had to adhere to. This had an immense impact on their psyche. Before the conversion, most of my grandparents' generation believed that they were 'Untouchable' and therefore not responsible for their lives. They were just born to be slaves, and to be of service to the Brahmins. The *Manusmriti* stated that if someone had died, it was the duty of the 'Untouchables' to remove the body. It also said that we were not allowed to drink from the common well, or enter any of the Hindu temples, for fear of polluting the Brahmins. But the conversion to Buddhism gave some of the *Mahar* people the confidence to take the initiative in their lives.

My grandparents managed to escape this life by moving from the village to the slums. They no longer lived on the edge of a Hindu community; they became part of a new Buddhist community. They were among the first generation of families who became part of the Dalit slum culture in the 1960s. So they took the initiative to escape the village mentality and search for a better life. But discrimination followed them, and Hindu conditioning had an effect on my father's upbringing. In our culture it is normal to live with your family, and so when my father married, he brought his wife to the slums. By the time my three brothers and two sisters were born 35 years ago, there were over 20,000 people in the slum.

Many families were unable to feed their children. My next door neighbour had five girls, a son, and no husband to support her. She lived in one room along with her mother and mother-in-law. She was the only one fit enough to go out and earn money for her family. She had no proper job, but managed to sell curds and feed her family with the takings. One of her children stole things and sold them at a nearby market, and another was already begging at the age of six. None of the children had clean or proper clothes or attended school. This was typical of many families where I grew up.

Most of us were born Buddhist. We chanted the five precepts weekly, but that was about all. Nobody in the slum understood the real meaning of the precepts or the *Dhamma*. Nobody ever explained to my grandparents' generation, my father's generation or my generation what Buddhism meant and how we were meant to practise it. All we knew was that if we ever saw a *bhikkhu* (a monk), we should have great respect and reverence for him. There were many pictures of Dr. Ambedkar about in the slum, but he was like a god: many of us worshipped him like one of the Hindu gods. In my home my parents always kept a fresh shrine with Dr. Ambedkar on it, and we celebrated the anniversary of the mass conversion to Buddhism on the 14th of October every year.

But my mother was still conditioned very much by the *Manusmriti* and the gods. She believed that women on their menses couldn't touch the family because the scriptures said so. When I was 13, all of a sudden my mother stopped me from touching any of the food or helping with cooking, or even helping myself to food. When we ate she gave me my food on a plate, making sure not to touch me. I was really upset and didn't understand what was happening, so I asked: "Why won't you let me touch any food in the house? I am quite capable of helping myself." She just replied: "It's because you have the menses, that's why." I was confused and wondered why I was unclean and polluted. I thought that because we were Buddhists all pollution had gone.

A year later, my younger sister fell ill and my mother had

to stay at the hospital. Because I was the oldest girl, I had to cook and clean for everyone while continuing with my studies for an exam. I managed to pass, and my sister came home well. However, when my exam results came through, my mother said: "I'm so happy my prayers have worked. You've passed because I prayed to the gods." I said: "No, Ma, I've passed because of my hard work." But my mother refused to listen. As far as she was concerned, the gods had heard her prayers. I have to admit that I've prayed to the gods as well. I always used to ask them to give me things. I laugh about it now, but it's true. Whenever I needed something, or something went wrong, I was down on the floor at the gods' feet, giving food and money and asking for their help. It's part of my culture. I did believe the gods had helped my family with some things.

I enjoyed my childhood very much. I played a lot, and hung out with about twenty other girls in the slums. I was also fortunate with my education, because I had a Christian teacher. She did her duty fairly. She wasn't like the rest of the teachers who never let any of us *Mahar* children represent the school or enter competitions. My Christian teacher encouraged all of us, no matter if we were high or low caste. I was also friends with a couple of Brahmin girls and even stayed at one of their houses on two occasions.

I knew I was lucky by the time I was 16, because most of my friends had been married. Very few of us did well in education. Most parents didn't have the money to educate their daughters. In the slums most parents believe that by the time a girl is 14 or 15, she needs to be married off. If she's not married by 18 they begin to worry that nobody will want their daughter or offer to marry her. Many of the friends I grew up with live in abusive situations with their husbands and in-laws. Those who are fortunate enough to work are making incense and selling it on the streets or working in alcohol factories.

I was able to escape this life because of my brother. He helped me get out of the slums when I was in my 20s. Although I managed to graduate with an MA in commerce and social work, because of great persistence and hard work, I was still trapped in the slums. But I was educated enough to know that marriage in itself was not a way out. My brother had become involved with the TBMSG, the first major group in Pune to help with educating the Dalits about Buddhism after Dr. Ambedkar's death. Their aim was to improve the spiritual lives of the Dalits, while also doing social work in our communities. My brother held meetings with people from this organisation in his home, and I was asked to help make the tea. I often listened in on their conversations and was impressed by what they were speaking about. It was unusual for young men not to talk about women. Instead, they spoke about the life and work of Dr. Ambedkar, and I soon became interested in him and Buddhism.

My brother joined the TBMSG and many Order Members of this *sangha* came to our home, and I felt inspired by their intellectual energy. At the same time, a close friend invited me to a meditation workshop, and from that moment I didn't look back. What was unusual was that in the slums everyone was in conflict, but although I was among people of the same caste in the environment of the TBMSG, everyone was smiling. I was inspired by the friendships and wanted to become more connected to these people. I began attending the programmes that TBMSG ran, and learned about Buddhism. I began to see why Dr. Ambedkar had wanted all the ex 'Untouchable' people to convert to Buddhism. I could see it had nothing to do with casteism, injustice or discrimination. It was about equality, morality and being a human being.

I became so excited by all this that I wanted to begin working for the TBMSG. I knew they had several projects running in

India. Part of their work is to set up hostels for children of poor backgrounds, mainly Dalits, from all over India. In 1992, the TBMSG set up one of its many hostels for girls in the State of Maharashtra, and I was asked if I would like to be a warden. I jumped at the opportunity. So I left the slums and moved to a new city to work with three other women to supervise the hostel.

This was exciting. I had the opportunity to help empower other Dalit children – and that's what I still do. We try to get rid of their conditioning by teaching them that education is important. We send them out to nearby schools, and when they return in the afternoon, we teach them about self-esteem, give them karate lessons, and encourage them to take the initiative through working hard at school. The hostels provide a safe, structured environment in which girls can develop and become different from the people they might have been if they had grown up in the villages or the slums. The hostels give the girls some autonomy over their lives. They know if they work hard at school they may escape early marriage. The parents only have to pay Rs 10 a month, so money is not an issue.

However, the parents do worry about their daughters' marriages, and we have to be honest about their achievements. If a girl is failing, the parents will often ask us to send her home, and she will be married off early. Many of these girls have huge regrets, and wish they had tried harder. The work of the hostels has improved so many young boys' and girls' lives, and many have gone on to do professional jobs, like working in the government, education and the medical field.

In the villages and the slums the situation is still critical. Most of these children still end up serving the high caste Hindus, or doing low demeaning work. Because of these issues, I began a project with some friends working in the slums. The issues in the slums have changed today. When I was young, we were only dealing with poverty, and with a few cases of typhoid, malaria, dysentery and leprosy, but these diseases seem to have become more prevalent in recent years, along with the new problems of prostitution and the spread of AIDS. Women often have no choice but to go out and sell their bodies, because their husbands have squandered all the money, and with tourism, prostitution has become a successful trade in some cities. But there is very little information about safe sex.

The slum communities have a lot to learn. Superstition still enslaves them and has a huge effect on how they treat people. For example, leprosy has become a great problem, and the community is not very good at dealing with this. Among the Dalit community we have created another 'Untouchable'. People with leprosy are seen as polluted and nobody will go near them, because they believe that if they touch anything that lepers touch, they too will develop leprosy. Issues of rape and sexual abuse have become more visible too in the slum community. Recently I was faced with a case where a three-year-old had been raped by a Dalit man. The three-year-old was attending the kindergarten I had set up with other friends in the slum area. When it came to my attention, I met with the girl's mother to see what we could do, and advised her to go to the police. But she refused because if people in the slum got to know about it, nobody would marry her daughter. However, the whole slum did get to know, so the woman packed up and left. This mentality is very typical of slum culture, and it's my aim to change such thinking. I want to help females of all ages who are subjected to such violence. Because of TBMSG I have been able to develop my work practice. It has supported me in going back into the slums and doing social work.

It is women who pass on culture, and so it's important to educate them about Buddhism. In the slums they are still totally dependent on the worship of Hindu gods for the provision of food and good health. They believe that poverty and illness happen because of karma. This makes the Dalit woman passive. We need to teach her that the health of her children, and money to provide food, can be created by her own hard work, and not by placing food and money at the feet of a god.

This is where the teaching of Buddhism is so important, and the Dalit community has waited too long to learn about it. It is time we took the initiative instead of waiting for another leader. TBMSG has given my community the confidence to embrace every aspect of our conversion to Buddhism. If all the Dalit people followed Dr. Ambedkar and believed his philosophy, we would change India; there would be a social revolution. I feel grateful that I was born into the Scheduled Caste; because of this I have found Buddhism. I am proud of and grateful to the community I come from and feel privileged to have found the TBMSG. I took *deeksha* a few years ago: I took on ten precepts and became an Order Member in this Buddhist *sangha*. I am not lay or monastic; I live out there in the world and try to help my community.

"Behind Every Great Man There is a Great Woman"

Ramabai first wife
She supported Ambedkar
Lost in history

I don't know how old I am, but I have seen many born and many die and my body is tired. My birth date wasn't important in those days, so nobody knows how old I am. But I am the oldest person alive in the village of Vananda who remembers the parents and cousins of Ramabai, the first wife of Babasaheb. Ramabai died in 1935 and I was living in the village with my husband and children when this happened. I never met Ramabai, but I moved to my husband's village, Vananda, as soon as we married.

When I came to the village, the people would not touch us 'Untouchables', and they would not step in our shadow. If my shadow accidentally fell upon them, they would scream, shout, run and take a bath. If I was thirsty, the caste Hindu people would refuse to give me water, and I would have to walk many hours for fresh water. If they were feeling kind, they would say to me: "Make your hands like a bowl." Then the person would stand as far away as possible and throw water, and whatever I caught I could drink.

Whenever there was a festival for the gods we were invited, but we had to sit very far away from them and they would only feed us rice and *dal*. This is the village that Ramabai grew up in. I didn't meet her because she was married to Babasaheb aged nine and went to live with him and his family in Mumbai before I moved to the village. But my parents-in-law knew Ramabai. They are related to her. I heard them speak about this girl who had left the village to live with Babasaheb's family, but I didn't know who she was till the day she died. My parents-in-law were very upset, and they gave her a special funeral, and my father-in-law conducted a special blessing on the tenth day after she died. I didn't understand why so many people were crying in the village, as she had never returned there to visit her family. My husband said: "Don't you know who Ramabai was? My uncle married one of her sisters, so she was my aunt."

After the funeral programme my father-in-law sat down with me and explained to me who she was. He said: "Ramabai is like your mother-in-law. She is a member of our family. We are one family together. I gave our daughter to Ambedkar, so our relationship is with Ambedkar too. Ambedkar is the person who is trying to end 'Untouchability'. He is the leader of our people." It was the first time I had heard of Ambedkar, and I was excited about what I heard. I also learned that after Ramabai's marriage it was not possible for her to visit the village because she suffered very much in childbirth, and had lost many children.

I never met Babasaheb either. But after hearing who he was, I felt inspired to go to one of the programmes he was holding in Dapoli. Many of us came from the village, because he was like one of our sons. I tried my hardest to get a look at him, someone even put me on their shoulders to see him, but there were many people there and I couldn't see a thing. So I just listened to his voice.

I remember when news came to the village that Ambedkar had been to the town, Mahad, not so far from here, and drunk water from the tank there. This was exciting for us, because we wanted to be able to drink from the same well as the caste

Hindu people in our village. Some of the educated people began to agitate in the village, demanding for us to be able to use the well. Some even rioted, and some of the educated high caste people gave in. They had understood Ambedkar's action and their thinking began to change.

A month later, I was walking past the well, making sure that my shadow didn't cast itself on the caste Hindu women who were waiting to fetch water. They called: "*Mahar*, come here." But I said: "No, how can I come?" And I walked on. A week later the same women were sitting outside their house, while I was walking to go and work in their fields. One of them called me and said, "Come and sit with us." I stopped; I was surprised. They beckoned for me to sit down, so I did, making sure I wasn't too close. One of them poured tea for me and gave it to me in a cup and saucer. I couldn't believe they were allowing me to drink from one of their cups. I wondered why they were being kind to me and said: "Why this change all of a sudden?" One of the lady's sons was sitting there. He was about 18 and he answered: "You and my people are no different."

Babasaheb's political action had a big effect in our village. Many of the high caste people began to change. They began speaking to us, even visiting our homes, and allowing us to eat with them at festivals. Many of my people began to insist on their basic human rights. I am very happy to be part of Ambedkar's and Ramabai's family. It makes me very happy that my house stands opposite where her house was. It makes me feel fortunate, and I don't want to leave.

Courageous woman
Heroine and champion
Rama his first wife

I came to live in Vananda in 1988. My mother's village was

extremely poor and many of the families who lived there did not have enough food to feed their children. So, when I was 18, my father said: "You have to be married. We can't afford to feed you any more. I will find a husband who can feed you." It was a relative who helped my father to find my husband. When news came that he was from the village of Vananda, my mother was excited because this was Rama's (Ramabai's) village. She was so happy that she agreed that the proposal should go ahead. She said to me: "If you go and live in this village, perhaps you will do good in your life, like Rama."

I had heard stories about Rama, how she had suffered very much and that she was a great woman, and was the wife of Babasaheb. Most of us knew about Babasaheb in our village, but it wasn't until I went to live in the village of Vananda that I began to understand who he was, and who his first wife was. When I moved here, my in-laws told me many stories about Rama – how her family was poor and how, when her mother died, at the age of 8, Rama took care of the younger children and helped her father with his fishing work. Since they were so poor, the father needed to marry Rama as soon as possible. This coincided with the time that Ramji, Babasaheb's father, was looking for a proposal for his 14-year-old son. Ramji found two possible proposals, but when he met Rama, aged nine, he was so impressed with how she looked after the household, the children and her father, that he immediately agreed that she should be his son's wife.

The parents of the other two girls were furious when they heard the news, because Ramji had suggested a proposal to their daughters, and they insisted he pay some compensation because he had shown interest in them. Ramji agreed, and managed to scrape together some money to pay for the harm he may have caused. In Indian culture, if a marriage proposal has been made to a daughter in a family and then it is withdrawn, it is very bad luck for that family. Many other families will refuse to offer their sons to this daughter because they will think that she is bad luck and that it was because of her that the first marriage never went ahead.

My father-in-law told me that when Babasaheb went to the United Kingdom to study, his son was very ill in India, but Rama decided not to send a message to him, because she didn't want to disturb his hard work. Instead, she decided to go out and work so she could pay for all the children's medicines. She walked for one and a half hours in the city of Mumbai looking for cow dung that she could make into small patties and sell at the market for fuel. Even when her son had a high fever, she would soak a cloth in salt water, wrap it around him, and leave him to sleep while she went out to work to earn money for medicines and for her in-laws. This was Rama's life, always thinking of her husband's work. It is said that she would say to him: "Our community needs your help; you must carry on with your hard work. You must study and do things for the community, as our people are not treated well. Don't worry about me."

Rama was very strong and courageous. There are stories of how her neighbours would insult her and say: "Your husband is educated and has a good job, but you have no good saris to wear or gold on your wrists, not even a *mangalasutra* around your neck to show that you are married." She would reply: "I don't need gold and beautiful clothes. My husband is doing good work. I choose to live simply." Babasaheb came to hear the malicious gossip, and made her a gift of many gold bangles to wear. But a year later he was struggling with money again, and didn't have enough money for a programme in Mumbai, where he was giving many lectures. Rama, said to him: "Here, take these bangles and sell them. I don't need them. Whatever you need for your community you take. I don't want your money. You just work for the community."

Rama is an inspiration for me. When I complain about my life, having to shell cashews and sell them to feed the family, I think of how hard she worked to look after her family. I want to be like her and support my husband, who does not earn much working as a conductor on a state bus. Many people seem to have forgotten how Rama supported her husband, but we are very proud of her in this village. The ladies' group often rejoice in her hard work. In this village we are all one family and we are all related to her. There are only 18 or 20 families and we all have the same last name, Dhurre. It is important to keep her memory alive.

But people are not interested in this village. We have no services here - no good roads, no toilets, and only two taps with running water. The women have to walk almost an hour to work in the fields. The nearest hospital is an hour away and the schools are all very far. We have no vehicles here and no bus service. There are no jobs here for the young men or women. A journalist came here maybe two years ago and wrote about how Rama's village was being neglected, and suddenly political leaders decided to pay attention during the elections. They promised they would provide facilities for us, but as soon as they were elected nothing happened. We had promises of a road, but nothing appeared. Two years ago students from the Ambedkar College in Dapoli united with some of us from the village to demand we have something better. At about the same time, Babasaheb's daughter-in-law came to a memorial for Rama here, celebrating her death on 26th May, and saw that there was only a tiny *vihara* to remember her. And so, a few months later, builders came to the village and began building a huge *vihara* with two big halls. Look at it. It's been standing half-finished for almost a year, and we've not seen a builder come back. People say there is not enough money to finish it, but I think that the high caste people have made it difficult to do anything here. They are jealous. They don't want to support this project and help the daughter-in-law to complete it.

I also think that because Rama was a woman, people are not interested in her life. We don't even know when she was born. We're not able to celebrate her birth because there are arguments over two dates. If she was a man or an educated woman, people would do things immediately. In my ladies' group we are doing our best to find out all about her life. We have begun to realise that if anyone is going to collect this information, it will have to be us.

Seventeen years ago there was absolutely nothing here to mark her life. People just said "This is Rama's village" and that was all. Then one kind man gave us money for a tiny *vihara*. Even today nobody pays any attention to the women of India. But slowly we are becoming educated, and may be something will change. I feel very sad, because there is still casteism against women in this country. Because Rama was a woman she is not important, and that is still typical of Indian culture today.

Ambedkar's Village
Neglected - Abandoned
Now a sacred site

The building we are sitting in now is Babasaheb's memorial home. It is where we keep some of his ashes encased in a *stupa* so people can come and pay their respects to our leader. His village is called Ambadave in the district of Ratnagiri. It's where his grandfather and father grew up. Although Ambedkar spent very little time here because his father travelled around with the army, it is family tradition that men take on the village of their fathers, while the daughters take on the village of their husbands' fathers.

When he was young he lived in Dapoli, a town two hours from here which is in the same district, and because of his family's traditional ties to Ambadave he often visited his family home as an adult. Once upon a time there was only a mud hut here, where his family lived. There were no roads, and no state buses that came anywhere near here. Even after his people converted to Buddhism there were no decent facilities. We had to walk 15 minutes for water, and if we needed any provisions that would mean a whole day's journey, two hours' walk to the shops and two hours back.

I had an auspicious marriage. In 1974, when I was 20, friends of the family introduced me to my husband. He was from Ambadave but I knew nothing about his village. I was born Buddhist, and my family always rejoiced in Ambedkar's hard work. I knew he had been an important leader for my people. It was a great surprise when I found out I had been living near his village for 20 years, and that I would be moving there as soon as I was married. I realised that I was fortunate that my husband's house was in Ambedkar's village. I could begin to take part in Ambedkar celebrations for the first time in my life. We celebrated his birth, the conversion and his unfortunate death on 6th December.

I learned a lot about his work and became very inspired by his first wife, Rama. Like many other women from the village, I was impressed by the support she gave to her in-laws and own family. Ambedkar's family were poor, and he didn't earn much money, but Rama managed to look after her children and make enough money for the whole family. In the early 1990s a few of us ladies in the village set up a women's group in honour of her name, 'Mother of Rama'. We came together because of all the work that needed to be done in the village. We first began to discuss Rama's work, and how she helped her husband's movement. We also discussed Ambedkar's philosophy and his speeches about women. Since then we have come a long way. We now talk about how we can help the movement and how we can become independent.

We have set up a small shop selling fruits and vegetables. In the early days of our group we set up a savings scheme, each donating Rs. 20 a month and providing loans to women who needed money. This has continued to be successful and we are able to help women to set up their own businesses, like sewing. Rama is the inspiration behind the many successes of the women living in this village today.

Ambadave has changed considerably since I came to live here over twenty years ago. There was some 'Untouchablity' when I first came to the village. We never shared food with the high caste people; we had no connection with them whatsoever. We lived in separate quarters, and we were not allowed to take fresh drinking water from the nearby well. I feel very sad when I think of the past, because even though most of the *Mahars* in the village had converted to Buddhism, the high caste people still treated us as if we were 'Untouchable'. But now we live our lives very proudly. Now there is no 'Untouchability'. We still live in separate quarters but the high caste people come to our houses and will sit down and eat with us.

In 1981 UNICEF provided money for a kindergarten, which was the basis for our village having a primary school and now a high school. And during the past 15 years people have begun to show an interest in Ambedkar's village, and to donate money. It has become a tourist attraction, which is good fortune for us. The government has provided us with our first set of toilets for the villagers, proper roads and a state bus which runs from the main town to our village every day. They've even given us phone facilities free of charge.

Many tourists are beginning to visit but we have no guest house to take care of them, and no place for them to stay. My village is the home of the leader of the Dalits and my women's group is campaigning to the government to provide something more suitable for our visitors. We would also like to see a library here of Ambedkar's work so that people will know what his life was about, and how he gave his whole life to the emancipation of 'Untouchables' and women.

Meera Ambedkar
Sheroe perpetuating
Babasaheb's legacy

I was declared President of the Buddhist Society of India in 1977, after my husband Yashwant Ambedkar died. I was in such great shock when he died that I wasn't even aware that I had been elected to this important role. When it was made clear to me that the legacy of my father-in-law Dr. Bhimrao Ambedkar had been handed down to me, I knew I had a huge responsibility ahead of me. My father-in-law had dedicated his whole life so that the downtrodden could have a human life. Now this responsibility had been passed on to me. Babasaheb (my father-in-law) wanted to take Buddhism into every slum and hut in India. His son Yashwant tried to do exactly this but unfortunately the people who worked with him were not interested in Buddhism. They were more interested in politics, and led my husband in the wrong direction.

When I became president I was determined that Buddhism should be in every corner of India. However I felt tense within myself because I still had four children at school and my husband was no longer alive to support me. I believed in Babasaheb's mission of educating children, and was determined that his grandchildren would not be ridiculed in the same way his son was. My husband was often criticised. People would say: "Your father was so well educated but you don't even have a degree. You're not following in your father's footsteps. What have you done for the mission? You are spoiling the image of Babasaheb's family."

I know that Babasaheb was so busy that he was unable to give undivided attention to his family, which is one reason why Ramabai, his wife, didn't survive, and why his son and favourite nephew weren't graduates. I wanted to remove this slur from the family, so I told my children after their father's death: "Whatever happens you must educate yourselves. This must be the first priority in your life." I am very pleased to say that all four children are graduates, in the arts, commerce, engineering, and my eldest son is a lawyer like his grandfather. While they studied, I gave my heart to fulfilling Babasaheb's wish of wanting the whole of India to be Buddhist. During the past 30 years I have had many volunteers helping me make this dream come true. Together we have set up training schools for women and men, teaching them how to conduct Buddhist rituals in the community. I continued the ten-day courses my husband had established for men who wanted to become monks, and also training courses for lay women.

Alcohol is a major problem in our community, so I have set up a training course for men with drinking problems. They are told that they have to commit themselves to a ten-day course, and if they attend all the sessions they can drink as much alcohol as they like in the evening. Many men sign up because they think it's a good way of getting free alcohol. However, after a day of Buddhist training, in the evening the men are asked to put robes on and go out into the community with a begging bowl. We tell them that when they return, we will fulfil our promise of giving them alcohol. After a couple of hours the men return, and we offer them a bottle filled with water, but all of them say: "No, I can't drink it now. I'm having an experience in my whole body that I don't want to change. I am wearing robes now. It's impossible for me to drink."

These courses have had a huge impact in the community and have helped to tackle the problem of alcoholism. In the last

29 years since I've been President, I have been working in 17 states of India and in 36 districts of the State of Maharashtra. I conduct at least 14 retreats a year, teaching people how superstitions, praying and worshipping the gods is corrupt and blind faith. These retreats have had such an impact that in north India some of the women who used to attend with their faces covered now turn up with their faces exposed and confident. (In some northern states women are not allowed to show their faces to their in-laws because of superstition.)

When I lead retreats all over India, I remind people that Babasaheb gave his whole life to make India Buddhist and because of him we are Buddhist, so we should not forget his great work. He founded the Buddhist Society of India, and conducted the great conversion on October 14, 1956, under the auspices of the society. It is my aim to walk in Babasaheb's footsteps and continue the great work of the Buddhist Society of India.

I think my marriage must have prepared me for this great work. I come from the ex-*Mahar* community, and I was born maybe 65 or more years ago in the Konkan. I grew up in Pakistan because my father was posted there to work on the railways. But after the partition in India we had to flee because of the many atrocities happening in Pakistan. Since my family had been in Pakistan, we did not know much about Babasaheb at all. In fact my father only knew who he was because of the many articles they were printing in the newspaper about him. I met Yashwant while visiting cousins in Mumbai. The husband of my cousin's sister-in-law was friendly with Yashwant, and it so happened that I was visiting when Yashwant was coming to dinner. I was asked to help prepare dinner for the guests. When Yashwant arrived, he saw me, and later asked about me. He was impressed with my cooking, and liked the look of me.

News of my proposal came to my family, and then I was told all about the Ambedkar family by my cousin's brother-in-law. I was appreheasive of marrying into such a famous family. It seemed like a big responsibility that I had not prepared for in my life. I was frightened of meeting Babasaheb, because once the proposal came I read as much as I could about him in the papers. That was when I began to identify with the struggle of the downtrodden. I learned so much through reading and discussing Babasaheb's work with friends and families.

I had been warned he could be short-tempered so I was not at all confident about meeting him. I had heard how he could look at people so intimidatingly that they would cower in his presence or leave the room. I married Yashwant in 1953. When I first met my father-in-law Babasaheb, I dared not look him in the eye, I would just inquire after his health and then sit in a corner of the room. I knew he was very busy and would not have time for me. However, I cooked for him whenever he came to stay in Mumbai. His favourite food was fish, and I delighted in sending a tiffin box filled with fish to his Mumbai residence.

He was a very generous man, and made sure that his son and favourite nephew never wanted for anything. He provided both our families with bungalows to live in. He was delighted when his first grandson Prakash was born in 1954. I remember him taking his grandson on his lap and playing with him at his birthday celebrations. Savita, his second wife, was even a little jealous and took Prakash from his lap and said: "I'm his grandmother. Let him have a chance to love me too." She took him to the Buddha in the room and placed a garland around him. Sadly Babasaheb never lived to see all his grandchildren born.

Yes, there is a mystery about how Babasaheb died suddenly, but this is family business. There are many rumours because nobody knows what happened, since nobody was allowed to enter the room on the morning he died. His cook tried to bring him early morning tea at 5.30 a.m., but his wife Savita prevented him from entering the room. Instead, at 9 a.m. she instructed him to ring Babasabeb's PA and tell him to come to the house. Nobody could believe that Babasaheb was dead. The PA was shocked because he was so well the night before, up working on the text of *The Buddha and His Dhamma* till almost midnight.

My husband heard about his father's death on the way to work. There were many people waiting for him at the station. I found out some hours later. I was disturbed by my neighbour, the principal of Siddharth College. I could hear him throwing furniture around and shouting. When I came out of my home there were many people gathered around our homes. The women began looking at each other as if to say, "Who is going to tell her this tragic news?" One of them asked if she could come into my house. I said yes, and then she told me the news.

It was a strange day, a day that changed my life, everybody's life. We were left with his mission. Although I didn't attend the mass conversion in Nagpur because of my two young children, I was fully aware of the conversion conducted by the Buddhist Society of India. When Babasaheb died six weeks later his son had to continue the mission and when he died 21 years later, I had to take the President's seat.

Now that my children have all left home, I can dedicate my whole life to the great work of my father-in-law. There are still many atrocities against my people. Caste Hindus still can't cope when families from the Scheduled Castes manage to uplift themselves. My role as president of the Buddhist Society of India is to take Buddhism into every home of India, so that casteism can become something of the past, so that all Indian people can live a proper human life, with liberty, equality and fraternity.

Notes

1. Caste / KEYNOTE by Mari Marcel Thekaekara. New Internationalist 380 July 2005) www.newint.org/features/2007/07/01/combatting_caste/

2. ibid www.newint.org/features/2007/07/01/combatting_caste/

3. Subhuti – Interviewee Buddhist scholar and author.

4. Wikipedia the free encyclopedia whttp://en/wikipedia.org/wiki/Purusha

5. Buddha and the Caste System, Bhikku U Dhammaratana, p. 5, pub-Jambhala Books, Pune, India.

6. Ibid., p. 5.

7. Vijay Mankar – interviewee - The Commissioner with the Ministry of Labour, Government of India.

8. Dr. Ambekdar, Annihilation of Caste, p. 39.

9. Mangesh – interviewee – academic from organisation Jambhudvipa.

10. Moon 1987, Vol 4, 230.

11. Daniel Gnanasekaran – CTC Bulletin. Dalits of Tamil Nadu and the Emergence of Dalit Theology – p.2 http://www.cca.org.hk/resources/ctc/ctc94-01/ctc94-01e.htm

12. Gail Omvedt, Ambedkar Towards an Enlightened Freedom, p.161.

13. Sonia Mahey University of Alberta, University Paper – source – Thind, G. S., Our Indian Subcontinent Heritage, Crosstown Press LTD British Columbia Canada www.arts.ualberta.ca/cms/mahey.pdf

14. Dr. Babasaheb Ambedkar Writings and Speeches, Vol. 17, part two, p.122.

15. Ibid., p.124.

16. Sadarshin Interviewee.

17. Dr. Ambedkar, Writings and Speeches Volume 17, part two, p. 126.

18. Manidhamma Interviewee.

19. BBC News online 2006 http://news.bbc.co.uk/go/pr/fr/-/2/hi/south_asia/6086334.stm

20. Dr. Babasaheb Ambedkar Writings and Speeches, Vol. 17, Miscellaneous Writings of Dr. Babasaheb, p. 118.

21. Sadarshin Interviewee.

22. Interviewee – Member of TBMSG.

23. Ibid.

24. Waiting for Visa – reminiscences drawn by Ambedkar in his own handwriting – published by the People's Education Society, p. 2.

25. Waiting for Visa, Ibid., p. 4, 5.

26. Waiting for Visa, Ibid., p. 5.

27. Vijay Mankar.

28. Sangharakshita, Ambedkar and Buddhism, p. 60, published by Windhorse.

29. Vijay Mankar interviewee.

30. Edited by Vasant Moon, Writings and Speeches, Vol. 17, Miscellaneous Writings of Dr. Ambedkar, p. 477.

31. Speech delivered by Ambedkar on October 27, 1956 – Why was Nagpur Chosen ? Section 12, Delivered from Hell.

32. Interviewee Sangharaskshita – Founder of the Friends of the Western Buddhist Order.

33. Ambedkar and Buddhism, p. 26 by Sangharaskshita.

34. Ratna – Interviewee PHD student on Dalit women's issues.

35. Maitranath Interviewee.

36. Broken People : Caste Violence Against India's 'Untouchables'. Human Rights Watch interview, Chennai, February 13, 1998, New York. Washington, London, Brussels, March 1999 by Human Rights Watch

37. Mangesh - Academic.

38. P. Laida ADECOM.

The **Arya Tara Mahila Trust** (ATMT) is a registered charity which helps women to help themselves. The ATMT supports women in India to alleviate the social problems resulting from generations of poverty. It has grown from 25 years of work amongst some of the poorest, most disadvantaged people in the world, those who were formerly known as "Untouchables".

Discrimination based on caste was technically outlawed at independence in India in 1947, but there is still widespread prejudice and women from the poorest strata of Indian society are especially vulnerable.

Indian women have created the new Trust in order to offer a context for social, economic and personal growth, inspired by a spirit of enterprise and independence. They are motivated by a desire to empower and enable themselves and other women to build effective projects which will fundamentally raise the quality of life of poor women in India.

The Trust aims to empower women to work together in non-hierarchical, participatory team-based projects in the social, medical and educational areas. Recent initiatives include a new computer institute run by women focusing on computer education for women and children from the slums, a project to help women deal with domestic violence, and small-scale business development based on 'trade not aid'.

Providing financial sustainability for the continuing work of the Arya Tara Mahila Trust and creating ways for women to earn a living wage is helping poor communities to move beyond the prison of poverty and social inequality.

If you can support this valuable work financially or in any other way:

Contact us at: atmt@vsnl.net;
tarahridaya73@gmail.com; atmt@googlemail.com
Visit our web page at: www.indiansisters.org
Phone: +91 (0)20 26611218